God in Control

Robert Gurney

Winged and horned figure bearing the name of Cyrus.

GOD IN CONTROL

*An Exposition of
the Prophecies of Daniel*

Dr. ROBERT M. GURNEY
M.B., Ch.B., D.T.M. & H.

H. E. WALTER LTD

First published in 1980 by
H. E. Walter Ltd
26 Grafton Road, Worthing
West Sussex BN11 1QU, England

© R. J. M. Gurney 1980

ISBN 0 85479 026 8

Printed in Great Britain by
Billing & Sons Ltd, Guildford and London

God in Control

ERRATA

Page 49, footnote :	Cf. Revelation 13:1; 17:3, 15.
Page 84, line 5 :	5:31)
Page 90, following line 36 :	. . . Darius annexed Thrace and large parts of Sind and the Punjab. He was succeeded . . .
Page 104, following line 21 :	. . . furthermore, that the Jews with Ezra had been slow to begin their task — just as . . .
Page 105, following line 6 :	. . . first asked for the restoration of the *temple,* and then he asked for the restoration of the *city* . . .
Page 123, end of line 29 :	. . . Luke 21:20,
Page 151, following line 20 :	. . . is *not* the Roman empire. Firstly, we learn here that Rome was badly defeated . . .
Page 153, line 33 :	. . . verses 39 and 40 . . .
Page 166, line 24 :	. . . (Hebrews 11:35b)
Page 186, line 16 :	Change 'apply' to 'only'.
Page 194, following line 19 :	. . . indicating that the end of the *present age* will be marked by increased apostasy . . .

Contents

MAPS

Preface

It is probably true to say that the prophecies of Daniel are the most remarkable predictive prophecies ever made. Not only are they astoundingly detailed and accurate, but also they look forward to the most important event in the history of this planet (if not the universe), and beyond that, perhaps, right up to the end of time itself.

Many Christians are fascinated by these prophecies and would love to know what they really mean; but they are confused and bewildered by the conflicting interpretations put forward in the past. Indeed there are some who feel that so many contradictory books have been written on the subject, it is useless trying to probe any further. Another book with a new interpretation would simply complicate the picture even more. The author feels otherwise. He believes that there is a real need for a radically new type of book which succeeds in sorting out this confusion.

This book has been written primarily for the thoughtful general reader, and it investigates the meaning of Daniel's prophecies in considerable detail. Although it takes a radically new line and contains many new ideas, it does also draw upon existing interpretations, both critical and conservative. It welds the various elements, old and new, critical and conservative, into a harmonious unity; and the result is, in the author's view, a distinctly clearer and more credible picture. It shows that the prophecies' *primary* fulfilment is in fact perfectly straightforward. And not only is it straightforward, but we can know it and be sure of it, virtually to the point of certainty.

The author is a medical missionary, and it is worth explaining how he came to write a book about Daniel's prophecies! It stems partly from his enjoyment of reading history and partly from his interest in the Messianic prophecies of the Old Testament. Although a conservative evangelical, he became convinced, some years ago, that the critics are correct in identifying Daniel's fourth kingdom as the Greek empire. This led to further research, further discoveries and the publication of articles in the *Theological Students' Fellowship Bulletin* (1967) and *Themelios* (1977). A further article has been accepted for publication in *The Evangelical Quarterly*. The author's qualification for writing this book is not that he is a theologian. It is the fact that he has made some new discoveries which throw fresh light on the meaning of Daniel's prophecies.

It has been a fascinating and rewarding study, pursued intermittently over a number of years; and the knowledge gained has been put to good use. The author is engaged in missionary work amongst Muslims — people who profess to accept that the Old Testament prophets were sent by God. He often raises the subject of Messianic prophecy when discussing the claims of Christ with Muslims.

Now critical scholars have done their best to reduce the Bible to a collection of ordinary human literature — and this includes the book of Daniel. They tell us that it (the book of Daniel) is largely fictional and contains many historical errors. Anything to do with the miraculous, they dismiss as spurious. The author has read several critical commentaries on the book of Daniel, and he has been sufficiently open-minded to see that they score over conservative commentaries in at least one area of interpretation. On the other hand, he has proved (to his own satisfaction, at least) that the critics have erred seriously in saying that the prophecies of Daniel are historically inaccurate.

Far from losing his faith in the book's historical accuracy and general trustworthiness, the author has gained added assurance that the entire Bible is the inspired Word of God. The prophecies of Daniel are only a small part of the Bible, but they have been attacked very heavily by the critics, and the confidence with which they have been dismissed as spurious and inaccurate is enormous. If the critics are wrong concerning the book of Daniel, therefore, we can be sure that they are seriously wrong in many other areas also.

The author prays that God will bless and use this book in spite of its many shortcomings. He would like to put on record his gratitude to all those who have helped in any way with its production. He is particularly grateful to The Rev. A. E. Cundall, Mr. A. R. Millard, The Rev. Stafford Wright, Archbishop Blanch and The Rev. J. E. Goldingay, all of whom took the time and trouble — at various times over a period of several years — to read the manuscript and give him their comments. He is also very grateful to the Rev. David Post, who drew the maps, and to his father, Dr. T. R. V. Gurney, who has helped in ways too numerous to mention.

CHAPTER ONE

Introduction

The Messiah

Christians believe that Jesus Christ is both Man and God, and the Saviour of the world. This belief depends to a large extent on the reliability of the New Testament documents — but not entirely. We have, for instance, a completely independent testimony in the shape of the Old Testament, a collection of writings formed long before Christ was born and held sacred by a people who are often hostile to the Christian faith. In these writings God promises that He will send a Saviour into the world — a God-Man known to the Jews as the 'Messiah'. 'Christ' means exactly the same thing as 'Messiah' — that is, 'the anointed one'. The former word is derived from the Greek and the latter from the Hebrew. Now Jesus's whole teaching was saturated with the claim that He was the Messiah. The following is an example:

> 'The woman said to him, "I know that Messiah is coming (he who is called Christ); when he comes, he will show us all things." Jesus said to her, "I who speak to you am he." ' (John 4:25, 26).

Again and again Jesus showed how He was fulfilling all the Messianic prophecies. The early Christian church (which was itself at first largely Jewish) continued to lay tremendous emphasis upon this when witnessing to the Jews.

> '. . . they came to Thessalonica, where there was a synagogue of the Jews. And Paul went in, as was his custom, and for three weeks he argued with them from the scriptures, explaining and proving that it was necessary for the Christ to suffer and to rise from the dead, and saying, "This Jesus, whom I proclaim to you, is the Christ." ' (Acts 17: 1—3).

The Old Testament builds up a very detailed picture of the Messiah, and the first piece of this picture can be found right at the beginning of the Bible, in the third chapter of Genesis. Genesis 3:15 seems to indicate that the first promise of the coming Saviour was given to the human race immediately after it had become separated from God by sin. The Saviour was to be a human being, a descendant of Adam and Eve. He was to crush Satan, but in the process the Saviour Himself would be hurt in some way. As we read on through the Old Testament, we find that He was to be a descendant of Abraham, Jacob, Judah and David. Although He would be born a man, He would also be God. He would be a prophet, priest, king and 'shepherd'. He would be the saviour not only of the Jews, but also of the whole world. He would be born of a virgin[1] and would come from Bethlehem. He would bring His glory to the regions of Zebulun (containing Nazareth) and Naphthali (containing Capernaum) by Galilee. He would come into Jerusalem as the Messiah, riding on the colt of an ass. He would be despised and rejected. He would humble Himself and unprotestingly allow Himself to be led as a lamb to the slaughter, and He would be killed. In His death He would be associated with both the wicked and the rich. He would suffer greatly, but in doing so He would be receiving the punishment due to *us* for *our* sin. His body would never see corruption.

These are only some of the Messianic prophecies.[2] In this book we shall be dealing with some of the others — those found in the book of Daniel. These latter prophecies are among the most amazing to be found in the Bible. They give us many details about Christ, but in particular, so the present writer believes, they predict the actual year of His coming, together with its setting in world history. These prophecies are like a great searchlight directed upon the Messiah and in its beam we can see the path of history which led up to Jesus Christ. The prophecies are full of rich meaning, but in this book we shall be dealing largely with only one side of them.

1.   The precise meaning of *almah* in Isaiah 7:14 is disputed. See articles on 'Immanuel' and 'virgin' in *The New Bible Dictionary,* Inter-Varsity Fellowship.

2.   Genesis 3:15; 12:3; 49:10; Numbers 24:17; Deuteronomy 18:18, 19; Psalms 16:10; 110:4; Isaiah 7:14; 9:1, 2, 6; 49:6; 53:1–12; Jeremiah 23:5; Ezekiel 37:24; Micah 5:2; Zechariah 9:9.

We shall see how the date and historical setting of Christ's arrival was accurately foretold long before His birth.

The early Christians were thrilled and excited by the way in which Christ fulfilled Old Testament prophecies. It is a vital aspect of the Bible's teaching and should be known and understood to some extent by all Christians. May we not be found worthy of the rebuke the risen Christ gave His two disciples on the way to Emmaus:

'And he said to them, "O foolish men, and slow of heart to believe all that the prophets have spoken! Was it not necessary that the Christ should suffer these things and enter into his glory?". And beginning with Moses and all the prophets, he interpreted to them in all the scriptures the things concerning himself.' (Luke 24:25—27).

The book of Daniel

The book of Daniel is a part of the Jewish scriptures which are known to us as the 'Old Testament' of the Bible. Its author claims (in the case of chapters 7 to 12, at least) to be a man named Daniel, a Jewish statesman, probably of royal blood, who lived and prophesied during the time of the Jewish exile in Babylon in the sixth century before Christ. The book contains, among other things, a series of prophecies which predict the course of history from the time of Daniel up to the coming of the Messianic kingdom of Heaven.

In the Hebrew Bible the book of Daniel is found in the third division, the 'Writings', and not in the second, where the prophetical works occur. This is because Daniel was not a prophet in the technical sense — he was a statesman who possessed the gift of seeing and interpreting visions and dreams. He possessed the prophetical *gift,* but not the prophetical *office.* It is interesting that another Jew who rose to high office in a foreign court (Joseph) possessed a similar gift — and in both cases it was partly because of their prophetical gifts that they *did* rise to high office.

The prophecies of Daniel are the chief Old Testament example of a form of literature known as 'apocalyptic' (apocalyptic features can also be found in other parts of the Old Testament, such as Isaiah, Ezekiel and Zechariah). The book of Revelation, in the New Testament, is the other major apocalyptic work in the Bible. Apocalyptic literature was very popular during the two centuries before the fall of Jerusalem in 70 A.D., and large quantities were written around that time. The relationship between the book of Daniel and these later, far inferior, non-canonical apocalypses will be referred to briefly a little further on.

The book of Daniel can be divided into two parts. Chapters 1 to 6 contain straightforward narrative material (for the most part), and chapters 7 to 12 contain prophetical or apocalyptic material. In spite of this division, the two parts are closely integrated (the first vision, for example, comes in chapter 2, thus forming part of the narrative section) and a common theme runs through the whole book — the theme that the God of Israel is the only true God and that He is far above all heathen idols, kings and empires. He is in control, and His ultimate victory is certain. His saints will be gloriously vindicated, but they must remain faithful to Him, whatever the cost.

The narrative section contains several stories which illustrate this theme. They are set in Babylon and involve Daniel and his three friends, and also three different kings — Nebuchadnezzar, Belshazzar and Darius the Mede. This narrative section will be referred to when it helps us to understand the prophecies, but we shall not deal with it in any detail. In this book we shall concentrate almost entirely on the prophetical section (including chapter 2).

The critical view

Now critical scholars claim that Daniel was not the real author, and that possibly he never even existed. They believe that the book was composed much later, in the second century before Christ, at a time when the Jews were being savagely persecuted by Antiochus Epiphanes, a Greek king. At this time, most of the 'predicted' events had already taken place. Thus most of the 'predictions' were not predictions at all — they were simply a record of past history. According to the critics, the book was concocted (perhaps with the inclusion of a certain amount of pre-existing material) for the purpose of encouraging the Jews in their resistance to Antiochus's persecution — and in fact the prophecies do concentrate very much on the Greek empire, particularly the period of Antiochus's reign.

It is certainly true that a very important purpose of the book of Daniel was to strengthen and encourage those who were persecuted for their faith in the time of Antiochus Epiphanes — and in all other times too. It reveals the one great true philosophy of history — which is that God is in control. Godless man may appear to be all-powerful; but God is in control. In His own time, He will destroy His enemies, and His saints will be vindicated and exalted. This is true. But to critical scholars, this is the book's only real value. As far as they are concerned, the book deals only with the time of Antiochus. There is no reference — of a *specific* sort — to the coming of Christ or any other future event.

They point out that the ascribing of a work to some well-known earlier historical person (a device known as 'pseudo-nymity') and the presentation of historical material in the form of predictive prophecy (although it was actually past history) were literary devices used quite commonly in those times — especially in apocalyptic literature. They suggest that it is wrong for us to judge this type of literature by modern Western literary conventions and to describe it as 'fraudulent'. They claim that there is no reason why a piece of literature of this type should not be included in the canon of Scripture and be regarded as 'divinely inspired'.

Up to this point, the critical argument may well be acceptable to some evangelicals. But the critics also claim that the book of Daniel contains many historical errors and that when the author does attempt to make some *genuine* predictions, they are completely wrong. In the view of the present writer, this latter aspect of the critical argument degrades the book of Daniel to the level of ordinary literature, robs it of any right to be regarded as 'divinely inspired' and is incompatible with the teaching of Jesus. Christ regarded the Old Testament as the Word of God and 'unbreakable' — and this view underlies all that He said and did. He repeatedly showed His disciples how it had foretold His coming, and He continued to do this *after His resurrection* (Luke 24:25–27, 44–47). Furthermore, He referred directly or indirectly to Daniel's prophecies on several occasions, and He applied them to Himself or to events which took place around the time of His first advent. His acceptance of the book of Daniel is shown both by His attitude towards the Scriptures as a whole (see,

for example, Matthew 5:17, 18; 22:29; John 5:46, 47; 10:35)
and by His references to the book itself, including the
specific mention of Daniel by name (Matthew 24:15).

Predictive prophecy

The critical argument fails to do justice to the importance
which the Bible attaches to predictive prophecy. According to
the Bible, one of the tests by which we can know whether a
prophet is true or false is that of seeing whether or not his
predictions are fulfilled. If the events he predicts do not come
to pass, we can know that that prophet was not inspired by
God.

> 'When a prophet speaks in the name of the Lord, if the
> word does not come to pass or come true, that is a word
> which the Lord has not spoken; the prophet has spoken it
> presumptuously, you need not be afraid of him.'
> (Deuteronomy 18:22).

This means, surely, that if the critics are right about Daniel's
prophecies, the author was a false prophet who was not inspired by God — and the book of Daniel has no right to be
included in the canon of Holy Scripture.

According to Isaiah, one of the things that distinguishes
the true God from false gods is the fact that God is able to,
and does, reveal the future through predictive prophecy. He
is in control of world history and knows both the past and
the future, right up to the end of time (Isaiah 41:21—23;
44:6, 7; 46:9, 10; 48:3—5).

This teaching is at the heart of the theology of the book
of Daniel. One of the things the book is saying is that because
God has predicted the future, we can be sure that He is
superior to the heathen gods and *He is in control.* If Daniel's
predictions are not genuine, one of the book's major arguments is invalidated — it is based upon false evidence. If God
did *not* predict the future, what guarantee is there (in this
context) that He *is* superior to the heathen gods and that He
is in control?

As we have agreed, an important purpose of the book of
Daniel was to encourage the Jews who were persecuted by
Antiochus Epiphanes. This was the first time they had been

persecuted for their faith, and some sort of encouragement was desperately needed. When the persecution arose, they found that it had been predicted by God long ago in the book of Daniel; and they were assured that it was all part of God's plan — *He was in control.* But if they had known that the prophecies were not truly predictive, they would not have got much encouragement from them. If the predictions are not genuine, the book loses much of its force and authority — it is little more than a piece of eloquent, but human, exhortation. It provides no real evidence that God *is* in control.

We know, however, that the Jews regarded the book as very much more than a piece of eloquent exhortation, because they accepted it into the canon of Holy Scripture. Although large quantities of apocalyptic literature were written between the times of Antiochus and Christ, none of it was accepted into the canon. The book of Daniel was given a unique place. If the Jews rejected the later apocalypses as unworthy of the canon, why did they accept the book of Daniel? Very probably the reason is that they regarded it as completely genuine. If they had known it to be pseudo-predictive, it is unlikely that they would have accepted it into the canon — except perhaps after a long period of time — and it is equally unlikely that they were deceived into thinking it was genuine when it was not. (If the Jews *were* deceived, incidentally, there is good reason to question whether the book has any right to be included in the canon.)

Although it is something of a digression here (we are discussing the importance of predictive prophecy in the Old Testament), we must add a word about another aspect of the book's message of encouragement. An essential part of this message was its prediction that although the forces of evil would appear to triumph, this would not be the end. God would intervene and establish His kingdom. Thus the book pointed beyond Antiochus to the coming of Christ and His kingdom. If we fail, like the critics, to recognise that the book really did point to Christ, we again reduce it to a piece of eloquent, but erroneous, exhortation.

Returning to the question of predictive prophecy, therefore, we have seen that the Old Testament attaches great importance to it. But so also does the New Testament — and Jesus

Christ Himself is its chief exponent. He often referred to the predictions about Himself in the Old Testament (e.g. Luke 24:25—27, 44—47). *A fundamental, vital and central aspect of Christ's teaching was His claim that He was fulfilling the Messianic prophecies of the Old Testament.* Furthermore, the New Testament indicates that these prophecies were specific and detailed — not vague and indefinite (e.g. Matthew 2:4—6; 4:12—16).

Jesus also made His own predictions (e.g. Mark 13), and one of the reasons He gave for doing so was very similar to the reasons given by God in the book of Isaiah (see references listed above).

'And now I have told you before it takes place, so that when it does take place, you may believe.' (John 14:29).

In saying that Daniel's 'genuine' predictions are erroneous, the critics are saying — whether or not they intend it — that the author was a false prophet who was not inspired by God. Jesus Christ, on the other hand, referred to Daniel as 'the prophet Daniel' (Matthew 24:15). This seems to indicate that He accepted the real existence of a prophet named Daniel and He accepted him as a genuine prophet of God. He accepted the book as a part of Holy Scripture, and He applied at least one of its predictions to events yet future at that time. The present writer believes therefore that full acceptance of the critical view of Daniel is tantamount to rejection of the teaching of Jesus.

Now predictive prophecy is a supernatural phenomenon — a kind of miracle — and whatever critical scholars may say to the contrary, they tend to make the assumption that 'miracles do not happen'. One of the reasons they give for a second century date of authorship is that some of Daniel's predictions are *so detailed and accurate* that they cannot be genuine — they must have been written after the events described had taken place. Predictive prophecies as detailed and accurate as this simply 'do not happen'.

But to eliminate every miraculous element from the book of Daniel, as the critics do, is gratuitous. There is a vast amount of evidence, both Biblical and extra-Biblical, that miracles *do* happen. And, furthermore, it is entirely reasonable and appropriate that God should perform miracles sometimes.

If He never revealed Himself in supernatural ways, how could we be sure that He is not a figment of the imagination? And concerning that supreme miracle, the resurrection of Jesus, the Bible itself says, 'If Christ has not been raised, your faith is futile'. (I Corinthians 15:17).

Daniel's prophecies are of a very specific and detailed nature. It may not be God's usual practice to reveal the future in the sort of detail we find in the book of Daniel — but the incarnation was not exactly a 'usual' event. The prophecies of Daniel look forward to the most important event in world history. And not only was it the most important event, but also it was a unique event. In order that He might redeem rebellious and lost mankind, God became man. God the Son put aside His glory and took upon Himself the human form and nature. Compared with this miracle, the miracle of Daniel's prophecies is small indeed. If these prophecies do indeed look forward to the coming of Christ, it is entirely appropriate that they should be utterly unique.

Historical accuracy and date of authorship

Now the critics say that some of Daniel's prophecies are historically inaccurate — particularly those which concern Babylon, Media and Persia, and also those which concern events after about 165 B.C. (when the prophecies were actually written). The former prophecies are inaccurate because they are about the distant past (relative to the time when they were written), and the latter ones are inaccurate because they are attempts at genuine prediction. Prophecies which concern the Greek empire up to about 165 B.C., on the other hand, are both detailed and accurate — because the author was writing about recent past history. Thus the closer the author comes to his own time, the more detailed and accurate is his historical knowledge. But when he passes over into genuine prediction, he loses all contact with historical reality.

These assertions form *the most important part of the critical argument for a second century date of authorship*. However, we shall show in the following pages that as far as the historical inaccuracies are concerned, the critical argument is completely wrong. We shall show that *all* the predictions are extremely accurate, even when they speak of events which took place long after the time of Antiochus Epiphanes — the very latest possible time of authorship (Antiochus died in 163 B.C.). We shall see that *events leading right up to the time of Christ are described in accurate detail.* To a large extent, therefore, the critics' main argument for a second century date of authorship is invalidated.

But even if this book does succeed in convincing the critical reader that all Daniel's predictions were accurate, he could still insist that the book of Daniel is a second century work. The fact is that neither the critical nor the conservative positions can be fully proved — yet. What we need is more evidence, particularly the kind of evidence provided by archaeology. As it happens, we do have some already. This evidence has not, so far, decided the issue one way or the other; but it has dramatically confirmed the truth of certain historical details in the book of Daniel, and it has led many critical scholars to suggest that the stories (chapters 1—6) came into circulation well before the second century B.C.

For example, critical scholars used to deny the historicity of Belshazzar because there was no record of his existence outside the book of Daniel. But then the archaeologists unearthed cuneiform texts which confirmed that Daniel was right after all . . . Dougherty wrote: 'The fifth chapter of Daniel ranks next to cuneiform literature in accuracy . . . The total information found in all available chronologically-fixed documents later than the sixth century B.C. . . . could not have provided the necessary material for the historical framework of the fifth chapter of Daniel.'[3] Archaeology has proved that the historical background to the stories in the book of Daniel is far more accurate than the critics realised, and it has provided strong external evidence favouring an early date for at least parts of the book.

Evidence of another kind has been provided by the 'Dead Sea Scrolls' of Qumran. The book of Daniel is well represented amongst the scrolls, and it is worth quoting R. K. Harrison on the subject: 'Since the community was itself Maccabean in origin, it testifies to the way in which Daniel was revered and cited as Scripture in the second century B.C. . . . That this

3. *Nabonidus and Belshazzar,* by R. P. Dougherty (New Haven: Yale, 1929), pp. 199f.

prophecy was unquestionably popular with the sectaries is evident from the number of fragments and copies of the book found in the Qumran caves. But since all these manuscripts are copies, and not the original composition, the date of the autograph of Daniel must of necessity be advanced by half a century at the very least, so as to allow the absolute minimum of time for the book to circulate and be accepted as Scripture.'[4]

There is much more that has been written, both for and against a second century date of authorship. But we cannot enter into all the pros and cons of the debate here. For further details, the reader is referred to other works by evangelical scholars.[5]

Apocalyptic literature

As mentioned already, apocalyptic literature (characterised by visions, lurid symbolism, pseudonymity, etc.) was very popular during the two centuries before the fall of Jerusalem in 70 A.D., and large quantities were written around that time.[6] There are certain very obvious similarities between this literature and the book of Daniel, and it is generally accepted that to a large extent it was actually imitating Daniel. Now the critical view is that the book of Daniel was written around the same time as these imitations. We should note, however, that apocalyptic features can be found in parts of the Old Testament other than the book of Daniel (particularly Isaiah, Ezekiel, Joel and Zechariah) — parts which even the critics agree were written long before the second century B.C. So the mere fact that Daniel's prophecies are apocalyptic in

4. *Introduction to the Old Testament,* by R. K. Harrison (Tyndale Press, 1970), pp. 1107, 1118.

5. See, for example, the chapter on Daniel in *Introduction to the Old Testament,* by R. K. Harrison, also the chapter on Problems of Old Testament History, particularly the section on the Captivity and Return, pp. 338—347. See also the article on Daniel in *The New Bible Dictionary* (Inter-Varsity Press, 1962) and the Introduction in *Daniel* by J. G. Baldwin (Inter-Varsity Press, 1979).

6. For an introduction to the subject, see *Apocalyptic,* by Leon Morris (Inter-Varsity Press, 1973).

nature is no reason for assuming a second century date of
authorship.

Furthermore, it is widely recognised that the book of
Daniel is vastly superior to, and in certain ways very different
from, these later apocalypses. It is, in fact, a distinctive
piece of literature in a class of its own. It is highly significant
that Daniel was accepted into the canon of Scripture, whereas
the later apocalypses were not. The book of Daniel has strong
affinities with prophecy and the Wisdom literature, and in
some ways it is 'definitely misleading', to quote Heaton, to
class it with apocalyptic writing. 'Daniel has suffered the mis-
fortune of being classed with his second-rate imitators.'[7]

If the non-canonical apocalypses are 'second-rate imitations', we can describe the book of Daniel as 'the genuine
article'. These 'second-rate imitations' are frequently pseudonymous and contain pseudo-predictive prophecy — but it is
completely unwarranted to assume that this must also be
true of 'the genuine article'.

Now 'pseudonymity' is the device of attributing a work to
some well-known hero of the past, such as Enoch or Moses.
But Daniel is known to us with certainty only from the book
itself; so it cannot be said that the book was attributed to a
well-known hero of the past. Hence it cannot be said that the
book is typically pseudonymous. Why should there be this
difference? In the light of the factors outlined above (including the author's special knowledge of historical details forgotten in later times — e.g., the regency of Belshazzar), there
is good reason to believe that the book of Daniel is not
pseudonymous at all — it was written by Daniel himself.

Jesus and pseudonymity

The author believes that if Jesus accepted that Daniel's prophecies were written in the sixth century B.C., then they *were*
written then. He finds it impossible to believe that God the
Son, who was in full communion with God the Father, could
have allowed Himself to swallow the idea that Daniel's astound-
ing prophecies were genuine when they were not.

7. *The Book of Daniel,* by E. W. Heaton (S.C.M. Press, 1956), pp. 35,
    37.

If Jesus was deceived by the device of pseudonymity, He was not merely deceived over a matter of authorship. He was deceived into believing that God had predicted the course of history hundreds of years in advance, whereas He had not. He was deceived into believing that God had mightily demonstrated His power — in the way described by Isaiah — whereas this was not so.

It is true that Christ was not omniscient during His life on earth; but this is very different from saying, as many critics do, that He could be deceived and could propagate error. Jesus plainly indicated that His teaching was both divinely inspired and infallible. The words that He spoke were the very words of God (see below).

As we have pointed out already, Jesus continued to explain to His disciples *after His resurrection* how the Old Testament had foretold His coming. Now it is safe to assume that after His resurrection, Jesus was free of the limitations He had during His life on earth. Did He modify or alter the teaching which He had given before His resurrection, when His knowledge had been limited? No! His attitude towards the Scriptures (including the book of Daniel) was exactly the same as it had been before — and no wonder. He had said, 'The word which you hear is not mine but the Father's who sent me'. (John 14:24). 'Heaven and earth will pass away, but my words will not pass away'. (Matthew 24:35). We repeat that if Jesus accepted that Daniel's prophecies were written in the sixth century B.C., then they *were* written then.

In Matthew 24:15 we read that Jesus said, 'So when you see the desolating sacrilege spoken of by the prophet Daniel . . .'. But do these words necessarily mean that Jesus believed in the existence of a sixth century Daniel? Almost certainly the correct answer is that they do mean this — unless it was common knowledge that the book was pseudonymous (because in that case the disciples would have understood clearly that Jesus was referring to a pseudonymous Daniel).[8] If there *is* any possibility that it was a well-known fact that Daniel was pseudonymous, then obviously there is a possibility that Jesus did not believe in a sixth century Daniel.

8.   Remember that pseudonymity was a literary device with which the Jews were perfectly familiar.

Now an evangelical scholar has argued recently that acceptance of a second century date of authorship is not incompatible with belief in the divine inspiration of Scripture.[9] Most evangelicals would disagree with this, but the fact is that evangelical scholars are recognising more and more the *humanity* of Scripture (without denying its divinity). The Bible is written in ordinary human language, in the form of ordinary human literature. Critical scholars led the way in recognising the humanity of Scripture — this we acknowledge — but they did so at the expense of its divinity — with disastrous results. A right balance must be reached in understanding both the divine inspiration and the humanity of Scripture.

The present writer believes that the device of pseudonymity was not incompatible with divine inspiration — provided it was not deliberately fraudulent and was clearly recognised for what it was by the original readers. But he finds it difficult to see how we can accept it in the case of Daniel. We have already given one or two reasons for this, but the most important one is that Jesus almost certainly *did* express belief in the existence of a sixth century Daniel. There is no evidence that He, the Jews, the disciples or the early church believed otherwise.

Pseudonymity and the coming of Christ

However, let us suppose for a moment — for the sake of argument — that evangelicals are mistaken, and that the book of Daniel *was* composed in the second century B.C. Should we, if the book were proved to be a second century work, abandon our belief that the prophecies look forward to Christ?

The present writer would answer this question with an emphatic No! Even if the book of Daniel were proved to be a second century work, he would still insist that it looks forward to the coming of Christ. And by that he would mean that it looks forward to the coming of Christ in a *specific* way — not in the rather vague and indefinite way allowed by some critics. It was not just an accident or happy coincidence that Christ fulfilled the prophecies.

9.   J. E. Goldingay, *Themelios*, January 1977.

He would concede that the book was written originally to encourage those who were being persecuted for their faith by Antiochus Epiphanes. He would even be willing to concede that the author may have *thought* that God's kingdom would be established immediately after the death of Antiochus. The author may have *thought* that 9:24–27 was entirely concerned with the events of his own day, and he may have *thought* that 11:40–45 described the last days of Antiochus. All this the present writer would be willing to concede.

He would believe, however, that *guided by the Holy Spirit,* the author actually pointed to the coming of Christ more than a century and a half later. He may not have appreciated the full significance of what he was predicting — but in the case of predictive prophecy, how can the prophet possibly understand the full significance of his divinely inspired utterance? That the prophecies of Daniel really do point to Christ will be shown clearly in the following pages.

The critical view is that the book predicted that God's kingdom would be established in its full glory immediately or very soon after the death of Antiochus Epiphanes. And since this did not happen, it follows (so the critics tell us) that the author was grossly mistaken. However, in this book we shall see that this view can be refuted simply by examining Daniel's prophecies very carefully and comparing them with the facts of history.

We shall see that Daniel did *not* say that God's kingdom would be fully established immediately after the death of Antiochus. Whatever the author may have thought, what he actually *said* was that it would be fully established after the death of Antiochus *and the total destruction of the Greek empire* (assuming 2:33 and 7:7 refer to the Greek empire). As a matter of historical fact, this destruction was a process which continued up to 27 B.C., only a few years before the birth of Christ.

The critics have been so engrossed in the details of their theory (that the book was written to help the Jews persecuted by Antiochus) that they seem to have completely overlooked the fact that Daniel's prediction *actually was fulfilled.* It is the critics who are mistaken — not the book of Daniel.

Basic assumptions

All books which deal with controversial subjects are written from a certain point of view and make certain assumptions; and this is particularly true of non-academic books. The present work is no exception; so it will be helpful if we indicate very briefly the nature of its basic assumptions.

These assumptions are based upon certain facts of history — facts which any open-minded person can verify, if he or she takes the trouble to examine the evidence. Our chief source of information about these facts is the New Testament, and the weight of evidence which it provides is far greater than most people realise. For example, it has been proved beyond doubt that the author of Luke and Acts was one of the best and most accurate historians of ancient times. It is very highly probable that he was a companion of Paul, and that he was personally acquainted with many of those who knew Jesus during His life on earth. He was an educated man, and in the prologue to his Gospel he specifically states, 'Therefore, since I myself have carefully investigated everything from the beginning, it seemed good also to me to write an orderly account for you . . . so that you may know the certainty of the things you have been taught'. (Luke 1:3, 4, N.I.V.). Outside the New Testament, supporting evidence is found in the writings of Pliny, Tacitus, Suetonius and Josephus, the Jewish Mishnah and Gemara and one or two other sources. There is also some archaeological evidence.[10]

These historical facts concern a unique historical person — Jesus Christ — and the main details are as follows. Jesus Christ was a Jewish teacher who lived from about 6 B.C. to about 30 A.D. He was born of a virgin in Bethlehem and was of the family of David, but He lived most of His life in Nazareth. He performed many miracles and claimed to be the Messiah. And by implication, at least, He also claimed to be God incarnate. He was crucified during the reign of the Roman emperor Tiberius, when Pontius Pilate was procurator of Judaea. He died on Passover eve, which was a Friday, and on the following Sunday He rose from the dead. As a result of

10.   A helpful book on the subject of New Testament reliability is *The New Testament Documents*, by F. F. Bruce (Inter-Varsity Press, 1960).

this event, the Christian Church was formed, thus changing the whole course of world history.

The present writer believes that if Jesus rose from the dead, it is reasonable to assume that His teachings are true, with all that that implies — including His deity and the divine inspiration of the Old Testament. It is also reasonable to assume that He enabled His disciples to produce a body of divinely inspired writings which incorporate a reliable record of those teachings (John 14:26 and 16:12—14 support this assumption).[11]

Now if the New Testament is divinely inspired, we should accept and believe what it says — and that includes its teachings on the subject of Old Testament prophecy. If we want to know what *God* meant by the prophecies of Daniel (and what could be more reasonable if it was He who inspired them?), we must pay attention to what He says about them in the New Testament.

As indicated already, *one of the most fundamental aspects of New Testament teaching* is the claim that Christ was fulfilling the Messianic prophecies of the Old Testament. However, we can show that Daniel's prophecies look forward to the first coming of Christ *even if we leave out the teaching of the New Testament, and even if we accept a second century date of authorship.* All we ask of critical or unbelieving readers is that they do *not* start off with the assumption that miracles never happen and that predictive prophecy is impossible.[12]

Daniel's prophecies

We shall turn now to the prophecies themselves and briefly view them as a whole before studying the details. The first two prophecies are revealed in two very similar dreams. In both of them, four great empires are seen to arise in turn, the God of Heaven finally destroying the fourth empire and setting up His own kingdom. The fourth empire is described in much greater detail than the others.

11.   A helpful book on the subject of Biblical inspiration is *Christ and the Bible*, by John W. Wenham (Tyndale Press, 1972).

12.   See *Miracles*, by C. S. Lewis, for a discussion of the philosophical problems of miracles.

In the first dream (chapter 2) Nebuchadnezzar sees a great image composed of four different metals. The fourth empire is symbolised by legs of iron and feet of iron mixed with clay. In the second dream (chapter 7) Daniel sees four great beasts. The fourth beast has ten horns, but then another 'little' horn grows up and fights against God and His saints.

In the third vision (chapter 8) we are treated to a description of the Medo-Persian and Greek (Macedonian) empires. The description of the latter includes a detailed account of Antiochus Epiphanes. The two empires are symbolised by two beasts, and of the two the Greek is described in much the greater detail.

The fourth prophecy (chapter 9) takes an entirely different form. In it Daniel is apparently given the exact date of the Messiah's arrival, together with certain details about His work and the subsequent destruction of Jerusalem.

The fifth prophecy (chapters 11 and 12) consists of two parts. The first consists almost entirely of a detailed account of the rise and fall of the Greek empire, and includes an elaborate description of Antiochus Epiphanes. It is preceded by a very short description of the Persian empire. The second part deals with a time of deliverance and glory awaiting the people of God.

Now the controversy over interpretation centres mainly on the first two visions. There are three main schools of interpretation.

1. The orthodox school. This school believes the four empires to be Babylon, Medo-Persia, Greece and Rome. The ten horns stand for kingdoms which exist during a second phase of Rome's history. It may be that they are merely able to trace their origin back to the Roman empire. The little horn appears during a third phase and may represent a man, government, coalition of governments, or an ideology. It opposes the saints until the judgment of God brings about the complete destruction of the Roman empire.

2. The dispensationalist school. This school also identifies the empires as Babylon, Medo-Persia, Greece and Rome. They believe there will be a revived Roman empire which will be divided into ten kingdoms and so the ten horns of the fourth beast are compared with the ten toes of the image — although

Daniel does not tell us how many toes this image has. This period, yet future, will occur after the return of Christ for His people. There are others who believe that Christ will return for His people *after* this period. The little horn represents a Satanically inspired prince of the revived Roman empire (the 'Antichrist'). This period will last seven years (the seventieth 'seven' of chapter 9) and will be ended by yet another return of Christ, who will reign on earth with His saints for a thousand years (Revelation 20:1–7). He will then withdraw and chaos will prevail until He finally appears for the third or fourth time.

3. The critical school. This school identifies the four empires as Babylon, Media, Persia and Greece (the Macedonian empire). The little horn is identified as Antiochus Epiphanes, a king of the Syrian part of the Greek empire.

The present writer believes that the four empires should be identified as Babylon, Media, Persia and Greece. Many people feel that belief in this interpretation is tantamount to acceptance of the critical school's version of the book's authorship. But this is not so. The present writer believes it to be highly probable that all the prophecies are genuine predictions and that the events described are historically true. (Incidentally, there were conservative Christians who held the 'Greek' view long before it was adopted by the critics.)

Let the reader consider, for a moment, the fact that critical scholars believe the fourth kingdom is such a detailed and accurate picture of the Greek empire that the author must have lived during the time of that empire after the events described had taken place. Clearly we must give very serious consideration to the possibility that the fourth kingdom *was* the Greek empire, even if we do not accept the critical version of the book's authorship. Evangelicals must not allow their judgment to be warped by their distaste for critical theology. We may not agree with the critics' view of the book's authorship; but this does not mean that they have nothing to teach us. Their observation that Daniel's fourth kingdom accurately pictures the Greek empire is perfectly valid. In fact one can think of several reasons (they are summarised in chapter 5) why Greece should be given greater prominence than Rome. Furthermore, at least one of these reasons should commend itself to conservative scholars *more* than to critical scholars.

One of the reasons critical scholars give for their belief in a second century B.C. date of authorship is the fact that the Greek empire is described very accurately and in much greater detail than the preceding empires. They claim that the author's knowledge of the Babylonian, Median and Persian empires is both scanty and inaccurate, and they point out various supposed errors concerning them in both the prophetic and narrative sections of the book. They believe that Daniel's first three kingdoms are supposed to represent Babylon, Media and Persia, but that his description of them is inaccurate.

Against this, conservative scholars have shown that there is good reason to believe that all the historical details in the stories are perfectly accurate. As we have said, archaeology has confirmed the accuracy of the historical background to such an extent that many critics now reckon that these stories came into circulation well before the second century B.C. — some perhaps even as early as the sixth century. In the present work we shall show that *the prophecies also* are completely accurate. In particular, we shall show that the 'four kingdoms' are an *accurate,* true-to-history description of the Babylonian, Median, Persian and Greek empires.

Now Daniel, like all other Old Testament writers, is ultimately looking forward to the New Covenant and all the glories of the Messianic kingdom — the New Israel. When Christ came, He taught that He was the Messiah, that the New Covenant is through His shed blood and that the New Israel, the Israel of God, is not an earthly kingdom, but is a heavenly kingdom whose citizens are drawn from all nations. The New Testament makes it quite clear that the kingdom of God was established at the time of Christ's first advent.

The present writer therefore believes that Daniel is primarily looking forward to the first coming of Christ. He describes how four empires will precede the kingdom of Heaven. God will begin setting up His kingdom by destroying the fourth empire (the Greek one) and He will strike the first blow in the reign of a particular king (Antiochus Epiphanes). In some very wonderful way, His kingdom will appear *after the total destruction of the Greek empire*.

In fact the Greek empire did begin to crumble at the time predicted, and Christ entered the world almost immediately after the final destruction of the Greek empire. Rome began her real conquest of the Greek empire (at this time consisting of a number of separate kingdoms) by defeating Macedon in 168 B.C. and the Jews began their successful war of independence in 167 B.C., all during the reign of Antiochus Epiphanes. Syria was annexed in 65 B.C., and the last vestige of the empire vanished when Egypt became a Roman province in 27 B.C. Shortly afterwards, in about 6 B.C., Christ entered the world to complete the process of setting up His kingdom. This kingdom is now undergoing a process of development, and a final consummation awaits it; but the initial establishment of the kingdom has already taken place.

(Note that the ninth chapter of Zechariah also seems to associate the coming of the Messiah with the passing of the Greek empire.)

Objections

The author has indicated that he believes the destruction of Antiochus Epiphanes and the Greek empire heralded the coming of Christ. He has also shown that the final destruction of the Greek empire *was* followed — almost immediately — by the birth of Christ. But, the reader objects, if the death of Antiochus and the destruction of the Greek empire were supposed to herald the arrival of the Messiah, why is there a gap of over a hundred and fifty years between the death of Antiochus and the birth of Christ? Why did it take so long for the Greek empire to be destroyed?

It is natural for us to feel that a rapid destruction of the Greek empire, followed immediately by Christ's arrival, would have been more impressive and convincing. But God's ways are not our ways — He does not do things the way we expect. (An example of this was the way in which Christ came as a suffering servant and not as an earthly, conquering, Davidic king.)

The period of delay may have been unexpected, but it was, in fact, remarkably fruitful. *A tremendous hope and expectation of a coming Messiah built up over the years after the time of Antiochus.* And this expectation was very strong — almost at fever pitch — around the time of Christ. This, perhaps, is one reason why Christ delayed His coming.

The rise of a Messianic hope was closely connected with the development of apocalyptic literature. And as we have noted, this literature was, to a large extent, inspired by the book of Daniel. It is likely that during the persecutions of Antiochus, people began to 'run to and fro' (12:4) through Daniel's prophecies as they saw his predictions coming to pass. A flame of Messianic hope was kindled in their hearts — a flame which burned ever more brightly as the years passed by. It is true that their concept of the Messiah was a mistaken one, but they *were* expecting Him.

Measured by the scale of a man's lifetime, a hundred and fifty years does seem rather a long time. But is this the sort of scale we should use? The book of Daniel describes history from six hundred years before the birth of Christ, and the Bible as a whole covers the entire span of human history — measured in many thousands of years. If we think a hundred and fifty years is a long time, we are getting things out of perspective. We need to stand back (mentally) and try to visualise the whole course of human history. Measured on this scale, a hundred and fifty years is actually a very short time.

Another factor which has to be taken into account is the phenomenon of 'foreshortening' in Biblical prophecy. Events which actually take place over long periods of time are sometimes squeezed together so that they seem to happen all at once, over a short period of time. We shall discuss this phenomenon a little further on in this chapter.

If the conservative reader finds the gap between Antiochus and Christ difficult to understand, the critical reader finds it even more so — or perhaps one should say that he thinks he understands it perfectly. To him, it is confirmation that the prophecies have nothing at all to do with Christ. The second century author was simply writing about the events of his own day. His prediction of God's kingdom was no more than a noble, but over-optimistic, hope.

To the critic, this is a thoroughly rational explanation which ties the whole thing up very neatly. In support, he cites the evidence for a second century date of authorship, including the book's tremendous emphasis on the persecutions of Antiochus Epiphanes. In addition, he asserts that some of the predictions which evangelicals say refer to Christ were actually fulfilled during the time of Antiochus (e.g., the prophecy of Daniel 9:24—27). Predictions which were *not* fulfilled around the time of Antiochus are dismissed as erroneous, and the fact that some of them *were* fulfilled by Christ is largely ignored.

What is our answer? We have discussed the question of authorship already, so this point need not detain us. We have indicated that the prophecies would still point to Christ even if a second century date were proved. We have also agreed that the book had a special message of encouragement for the Jews who suffered under Antiochus.

But how do we explain the fact that some of the predictions about Christ were also fulfilled (apparently) around the time of Antiochus? This is not an easy question to answer, but we can begin by noting that the events of Antiochus's reign fulfilled these predictions *imperfectly,* whereas those of Christ's time fulfilled them *perfectly.* A possible (but highly unlikely) explanation is that the book was, as the critics say, written in the second century B.C. The author *thought* that he was writing about his own time only; but guided by the Holy Spirit, he was actually pointing forward to the coming of Christ.

But what if the book of Daniel is a work of the sixth century? We emphasise that these prophecies (9:24—27 and 12:1—3, 7) were fulfilled *perfectly* by the coming of Christ and the destruction of Jerusalem in 70 A.D., but *imperfectly* in the time of Antiochus. There is a superficial similarity between the events of Antiochus's reign and the events described in 9:26, 27 and 12:7, but there is very little, if any, correspondence with the other parts of these prophecies (9: 24, 25 and 12:1—3) — these parts were fulfilled by Christ, and Christ alone.

The similarities could be passed off as a coincidence, but there seems to be more to it than this. As we shall see, Christ Himself applied the prophecy of 9:26b, 27b to the events of 70 A.D., but He also seemed to link it with the persecution of Antiochus (which preceded His first advent) and the tribulation which is to precede His second advent. The primary reference is to the events of 70 A.D., but there seems to be some sort of secondary reference to the 'tribulation' which

preceded the first advent and to another one which will precede the second advent. (This problem of 'primary' and
'secondary' fulfilments is discussed a little further on in this
chapter.)

The author cannot help feeling also that part of the answer
may be that Daniel's prophecies are something of a riddle —
and that God made it this way deliberately. Jesus sometimes
obscured His message by speaking in parables — and He did it
deliberately, for a reason (Matthew 13:10—17). In other words
these predictions were deliberately inspired by God in such a
way that people can avoid seeing that they point to Christ. If
a person has decided the issue in advance, there are some things
that he simply does not want to see — and God does not force
people to see the truth against their wills. If the reader finds
this idea difficult to accept, he should look up the passage we
have just referred to (Matthew 13:10—17). The way in which
some of Daniel's predictions about Christ *appear* to apply to
the time of Antiochus provides an easy way out for those who
do not want to believe. But in the present writer's humble
opinion, these people are deceiving themselves.

It is easy to feel that God would have done better to have
made these predictions absolutely plain and obvious. But we
repeat that His ways are not our ways. He does not always lay
everything on a plate before us — He wants us to search for
the truth. The kingdom of Heaven is like hidden treasure
(Matthew 13:44). If we approach the subject with truly open
minds, with attitudes of belief and expectation, and of respect
for God's Word, our search will be rewarded. 'Seek, and you
will find; knock, and it will be opened to you' (Matthew 7:7).

Doubts and uncertainties

Now a good many readers, both critical and conservative, will
disagree already with much of what has been said so far. And
the author acknowledges that the whole subject is highly
controversial and that it is unwise to be dogmatic.

Although the New Testament lays great stress on the fact
that many things about Christ were prophesied in the Old
Testament, it does make it plain that the prophecies are not
crystal clear in meaning. The Jewish people as a whole did
not understand them, and most of them did not recognise

Christ when He came. Even the disciples of Jesus were slow to understand. And even with our present knowledge of Christ, with the advantage of hindsight, it is still possible for Bible-believing Christians of equal sincerity to differ over the interpretation of some parts.

Having thus cautiously admitted the controversial nature of the subject and the inadvisability of being dogmatic, the author will now proceed to stick his neck out slightly further. The interpretation expounded in the following pages is largely concerned with *known facts of past history*. Clearly, such an interpretation is capable of a greater degree of proof than interpretations concerned with the unknown future. The author himself feels that Daniel's prophecies apply so perfectly to events preceding and immediately following Christ's first advent, he has a considerable degree of confidence in the correctness of this interpretation. However, he does feel that these past events undoubtedly *typify*, at least, certain events yet to come. Whether the prophecies will find more specific fulfilment than this in the future is a matter for debate and conjecture. It may or may not be so. Time will tell.

It seems that some predictive prophecies in the Bible had primary fulfilments which took place soon after the prophecies were given, but also more distant secondary fulfilments. It is possible that Daniel's prophecies are of this type. We suggest that if they are, the interpretation expounded in this book is the primary fulfilment, and the secondary fulfilment is the one that is yet to come. The author does indicate in the final chapter of this book what sort of secondary application he prefers, but he is not dogmatic about it — he acknowledges the possibility that there may be a future fulfilment more specific than that which he suggests. He maintains, however, that even if there is such a future fulfilment, it will be a secondary one which need not alter in any way the primary fulfilment expounded in the following pages.

In connection with this question of 'primary and secondary' fulfilments, it is worth reminding ourselves here that apart from the books of Luke and Acts, the entire Bible was written by Jews. And Jesus Himself was a Jew. If we are to understand the Bible fully, therefore, it is sometimes necessary for us to see it through the eyes of the Hebrew. People often get very perplexed and confused over the question of whether

Daniel's prophecies look forward to the first advent or the second advent, and whether Jesus was referring (in Matthew 24) to 70 A.D. or to His second advent. In fact Jesus was probably referring to both events at one and the same time — and it may well be that this was perfectly natural to Hebrew thought. Although separated by hundreds of years, these two happenings are a *single event*. Daniel's prophecies look forward to the first advent *and* the second advent. The prediction of Israel's punishment in Deuteronomy 28 looks forward to Nebuchadnezzar's siege *and* the siege of 70 A.D. Let us remember that Daniel's prophecies come to us from the East, and that they do not necessarily conform to the Western concept of time. (I am indebted to Martin Goldsmith, a Hebrew Christian, for this insight.)

In Biblical predictive prophecy, therefore, events which are separated by long periods of time are sometimes telescoped together in such a way that they seem to be (because in one sense they *are*) one event. Likewise, events which take place over long periods of time are sometimes squeezed together or 'foreshortened' (like a range of mountains viewed from a distance) in such a way that they seem to happen all at once. Daniel saw that God's kingdom would be established at a certain point of time in world history, and he saw that it would fill the earth and have absolute dominion. But he did not see that many centuries were to elapse between the founding of the kingdom and the time when it would, in every sense of the phrase, 'fill the whole earth'. (Likewise he did not see that a number of years were to elapse between the death of Antiochus Epiphanes and the final destruction of the Greek empire.)

We believe, therefore, that Daniel's prophecies look forward to the first coming of Christ, but they look beyond it to the second coming also. They *were* fulfilled by the first coming, to a large extent; but it is only when Christ returns at the end of this age — when God destroys the present universe and creates 'a new heaven and a new earth' (Revelation 20:11; 21:1) — that the fulfilment will be total and complete.

Times and numbers

Before concluding this chapter, the author would like to say a few words about the vexed question of 'times and numbers' in the book of Daniel. Daniel's prophecies contain references to certain mysterious measurements of time, together with cryptic numbers, which have always been a cause of some confusion. The tendency amongst evangelical scholars is to assume that these numbers and units of time are entirely symbolical and are not to be taken literally.

The present writer agrees that these numbers are highly symbolical, but as far as he can see, there is no good reason why they should not have a literal significance also. In the case of the 'seventy weeks' (9:24—27), for example, we shall see that there *was* a literal fulfilment; but at the same time, the number seventy does have a symbolic significance.

Another period of time which crops up more than once, but in different forms, is that of three and a half years. The figure three and a half has a definite symbolic significance, yet at the same time it is a fact that Antiochus's persecution did last for approximately three and a half years — as did the public ministry of Jesus and the Jewish War of 67—70 A.D. We shall deal with the literal aspect of these 'times and numbers' as we encounter them, but their symbolic significance will be dealt with in the final chapter.

In one case, incidentally, the numbers seem to serve the purpose of helping us to distinguish between different historical events which might otherwise be confused with each other. In 7:25 we are told that Antiochus's persecution lasted three times and part (*pelag*) of a time. In 12:7, however, mention is made of a period of three times and half (*chatsi*) a time. The difference is small, but as we shall see, it indicates that these verses describe two completely different events. In the former case it is Antiochus's persecution, and in the latter it is the Jewish War of 67—70 A.D.

Conclusion

The author would like to emphasise again that in this book he does not deal with every aspect of Daniel's prophecies. He concentrates mainly on showing that the historical predictions were accurate, and that they foretold the date and historical setting of Christ's first coming. However, he does also relate the prophecies to the age in which we are living now. He does this in the final chapter, mainly; but also, to some extent, throughout the book.

Several issues have been raised in this introduction, not all of which have been dealt with very thoroughly; but enough has been said for this book's purpose. (For a more thorough treatment of some of these issues, see *Introduction to the Old Testament,* by R. K. Harrison, and *Daniel,* by J. G. Baldwin.) So without further ado, let us now examine the prophecies in detail.

CHAPTER TWO

The Image

In the second chapter of Daniel we read about the dream in which a great image represents four great kings or kingdoms. The dream is dreamed by Nebuchadnezzar, king of Babylon, and the interpretation is given by Daniel.

This prophecy and the parallel one of the four beasts are recorded in the Aramaic language and not in Hebrew. In fact the whole section 2:4 to 7:28 is in Aramaic, an international Gentile tongue. This is appropriate, because both visions deal with the rising and falling of great Gentile nations and the ultimate triumph of God's people over them.

Nebuchadnezzar receives the revelation in the second year of his reign. Because he has forgotten the dream and is determined to learn the real truth, he calls upon his wise men to describe the dream itself as well as its interpretation. This they are unable to do. But Daniel and his companions pray to God and the secret is revealed to Daniel in a 'vision of the night'. This is how he describes it to the king:

'. . . there is a God in heaven who reveals mysteries, and he has made known to King Nebuchadnezzar what will be in the latter days. Your dream and the visions of your head as you lay in bed are these: To you, O king, as you lay in bed came thoughts of what would be hereafter, and he who reveals mysteries made known to you what is to be. But as for me, not because of any wisdom that I have more than all the living has this mystery been revealed to me, but in order that the interpretation may be made known to the king, and that you may know the thoughts of your mind.

'You saw, O king, and behold, a great image. This image, mighty and of exceeding brightness, stood before you, and its appearance was frightening. The head of this image was

of fine gold, its breast and arms of silver, its belly and thighs of bronze, its legs of iron, its feet partly of iron and partly of clay . . .' (Daniel 2:28—33).

The head of gold

The image has a head of gold, and Daniel interprets it as follows:

'*You, O king, the king of kings, to whom the God of heaven has given the kingdom, the power, and the might, and the glory, and into whose hand he has given, wherever they dwell, the sons of men, the beasts of the field, and the birds of the air, making you rule over them all — you are the head of gold.' (Daniel 2:37, 38).*

Thus we are told that the head of gold represents *Nebuchadnezzar*, king of Babylon. Under Nebuchadnezzar, Babylon rose to a position of great power, wealth and magnificence.

The breast and arms of silver

The breast and arms of this image are of silver and Daniel interprets as follows:

'*After you shall arise another kingdom inferior to you . . .' (Daniel 2:39a).*

In the present writer's opinion, Daniel is here describing the Median empire. This empire was contemporaneous with the Babylonian empire, but after the death of Nebuchadnezzar in 562 B.C. *it became the stronger of the two,* because the power and wealth of Babylon immediately declined. Babylon was still a power, but the scales had tipped in favour of the Medes. Remember that the head of gold symbolises Nebuchadnezzar and Daniel says, 'After *you* (Nebuchadnezzar) shall arise another kingdom inferior to *you*'. Following the death of Nebuchadnezzar, Media was the major power for at least twelve years until it was united with Persia in 550 B.C. under the rule of Cyrus. The Median empire did not, however, have the glory and magnificence of Nebuchadnezzar's Babylon — it was of *inferior* quality.

The usual objection to this is that the Median empire did not follow after the Babylonian empire — it was contemporaneous with it. It may be replied, however, that the order of Daniel's kingdoms is the order of their rise to the height of power and prominence. Daniel does not say that each kingdom exists only from the time of destruction of the preceding kingdom to the time of its own destruction. The order of the kingdoms is *not* merely the order of their existences — it is the order of their occupation of the seat of supreme power. In other words, the order in which they held the title of 'top nation'! This is confirmed in the vision of the four beasts, because we learn there that after the fourth kingdom has been destroyed, the first three kingdoms continue to exist for a while *together,* although their dominion is taken away from them. This clearly indicates that they are to some extent contemporaneous.

The assertion that there was no Median empire between the Babylonian and Persian empires seems to be based on a misconception. This misconception is the idea that Persia succeeded Babylon as dominant world power when it overthrew Babylon in 539 B.C. Persia became the dominant world power some years *before* Babylon fell. Cyrus built up a very large and powerful empire which outstripped the Babylonian empire several years before he got round to conquering the latter empire. If it be admitted, and so it must, that Persia became the dominant world power before the actual fall of Babylon, it can also be admitted that Media may have been the dominant world power before Persia.

It will probably be objected that the Jews had little or nothing to do with the Median empire. This is not only irrelevant; it is also largely incorrect. Both visions describing the four kingdoms are recorded in Aramaic, a Gentile tongue. This could suggest that these first two visions give a *world-view* of earth's kingdoms — not a narrow Jewish view. The later prophecies do tend to concentrate more on the Jewish view; but not so much these first two prophecies. In any case, the Jews *were* very conscious of the Median empire. That empire and the Babylonian one were the two great rivals for world power, and every educated Jew in the major centres of communication, like Babylon, would have been acutely conscious of the former's existence. This was the situation when Nebuchadnezzar saw his vision of the image. When Daniel saw the vision of the four beasts (after Nebuchadnezzar's death), Media loomed even larger. In fact those who knew the prophecies of Isaiah and Jeremiah (see following chapter) had always expected Media to overthrow Babylon. This was the state of affairs for a few uneasy years. But suddenly, events took an unexpected turn. Media's king was overthrown by one of his own vassals, the brilliant Persian king, Cyrus. This man, who was related to the royal house of Media either by descent or marriage, began his climb to the seat of supreme power from the throne of the small Persian kingdom of Anshan. He united the Medes and Persians as allies under his own rule; but from this time Persia was on the ascendant. For some years the two peoples held the reins of power together; but the Persians had the edge on the Medes and increased their power until they were completely dominant.

The belly and thighs of bronze

Daniel continues the interpretation as follows:

> '. . . and yet a third kingdom of bronze, which shall rule over all the earth.' (Daniel 2:39b)

The third kingdom is symbolised by the image's belly and thighs of bronze and is to 'rule over all the earth'. The characteristic of this third kingdom is the immense area over which it rules. This is a perfect description of the Persian empire, because the most striking aspect of that empire was the huge area it covered — it was by far the vastest empire the world had seen. The following Greek empire was in fact slightly smaller than the Persian empire. In all regions except Greece and across the Indus river, Alexander's Greek empire either fell short of or failed to extend beyond the limits of the Persian empire.

Cyrus himself created the largest empire the world had seen up to that time; but his successors continued to push the frontiers outwards until the Persian empire was truly breathtaking in size. In a series of brilliant campaigns Cyrus annexed the entire Median empire, the large and powerful kingdom of Lydia in Asia Minor, much territory in the East — and then the Babylonian empire. His successors added all Egypt, a chunk of Europe and more territory in the East.

Note that the references to Cyrus in Isaiah and elsewhere indicate that in the Biblical view, Cyrus the Persian was far from 'inferior'. Note also the way in which Daniel groups together the second and third kingdoms. The second kingdom is passed over quickly with a brief and belittling remark, possibly indicating that its term of supreme power is comparatively insignificant and short-lived, as well as being inferior in wealth and magnificence. It is grouped with, and closely followed and overshadowed by, the world-ruling third kingdom. The whole description is strongly suggestive of the Medo-Persian situation, because the comparatively insignificant Median empire was absorbed and eclipsed by the subsequently enormous Persian empire only a very short time after it (Media) had itself surpassed Babylon. The description of the second and third kingdoms fits the Median and Persian empires far better than it fits the huge, wealthy, long-lived Persian empire and the rather smaller Greek empire.

The legs of iron, and feet of iron and clay

The fourth empire is symbolised by the legs of iron and feet of iron and clay. Daniel explains,

> '*And there shall be a fourth kingdom, strong as iron, because iron breaks to pieces and shatters all things; and like iron which crushes, it shall break and crush all these. And as you saw the feet and toes partly of potter's clay and partly of iron, it shall be a divided kingdom; but some of the firmness of iron shall be in it, just as you saw iron mixed with the miry clay. And as the toes of the feet were partly iron and partly clay, so the kingdom shall be partly strong and partly brittle. As you saw the iron mixed with miry clay, so they will mix with one another in marriage, but they will not hold together, just as iron does not mix with clay.*' (Daniel 2:40—43)

This is a perfect description of the Macedonian Greek empire. The legs of iron represent that empire in the time of Alexander the Great. Her power was irresistible and utterly phenomenal. She smashed the power of Persia rapidly and completely. The fall of Tyre with the savage treatment of its inhabitants struck terror into the heart of the East. Alexander is possibly

the greatest military genius the world has ever known. He
made war as no man in the world before. He was supreme in
strategy, tactics and organisation, swift and sure to strike. All
resistance was swept away before him and he never knew defeat. Setting out from Greece in 334 B.C., his army stormed
through the East like a whirlwind, his disciplined troops finding none to resist them effectively. Even today there are
traces of the many legends that gathered around that terrible
name.

But then in 323 B.C., at the age of 33, Alexander died a
premature and tragic death — before he was able to organise
his empire into as closely cohesive a system as that of the
Persians. And so the empire was divided between his generals.
Immediately it was weakened, divided and at strife within
itself. The feet of iron and clay therefore represent the
period following the death of Alexander. Now this extraordinary man had initiated a plan to fuse East and West
under one Hellenic culture by means of a policy of inter-
marriage and the planting of numerous Greek colonies all over
his empire. These colonies were communities of Greek people
carrying on the Greek way of life in the midst of an alien
environment. 'They shall mingle themselves with the seed of
men', as the R.V. translates it, is a very apt description of
this deliberate policy of integration. The iron-like strength of
Alexander's Greece was broken up and mingled with the clay-
like weakness of the conquered peoples, but the complete
fusion that Alexander had visualised never came to fruition —
'they will not hold together, just as iron does not mix with
clay'. In the Egyptian section of the divided empire particularly, there was a complete and utter failure of the Greeks to
fuse with the native people though there was some degree of
fusion in the Syrian part of the empire.

The generals who succeeded Alexander founded separate
Greek dynasties which continued to rule over the various
fragments of the empire. These dynasties always remained
essentially Greek and were not absorbed by the nations they
ruled. They were constantly at strife with each other, first
one side being the stronger and then the other. Much of
Daniel 11 is taken up with an account of their struggles and
unsuccessful attempts at reconciliation. The result of all this

was a weak and divided empire which contained elements of the original Greek strength.

One of the most enthusiastic supporters of the policy of amalgamating Greek and barbarian was Antiochus Epiphanes, a descendant of one of Alexander's generals and king of the eastern part of the Greek empire. He sought to unite his empire of many different races by giving them one Hellenic culture and religion. His most notable failure was his effort to absorb the Jewish people. A considerable proportion of them stoutly refused to mingle with the Greek 'iron'. In order to make them conform, Antiochus had to resort to force, and the result was a savage persecution of those who remained faithful to Judaism. It is with this persecution that much of chapters 7, 8 and 11 are concerned.

It can be seen, therefore, that the post-Alexandrian Greek empire fulfils all the various similes of the iron and clay — the empire was divided, it contained some of the original strength, it was partly strong and partly broken and the Greeks 'mingled themselves with the seed of men' without cleaving to them. The Alexandrian Greek empire, on the other hand, by its irresistible strength completely fulfilled the prophecy of the legs of iron.

Rome was strong, but her strength was of a different nature. She was not irresistible — she lost battles. Her empire grew slowly and almost reluctantly. She did not by any means 'shatter all things'. Alexander defeated everyone he fought; but Rome was unable, for instance, to overcome the Parthians. At one stage, in fact, the Parthians drove the Romans right out of Palestine. The failure of Rome against Parthia is specifically mentioned later in the book of Daniel (11:44, 45).

In his book, *A History of Warfare,* Lord Montgomery says some very significant things about the Greek and Roman armies. Describing the army of Alexander, he says, 'The net result was the best balanced and most powerful army of ancient times — an army equipped to fight in any type of country and against any enemy. The essence of the Macedonian technique of warfare under Alexander was the combination of the rock-like phalanx with light and heavy cavalry'. About the Roman armies, he says, '. . . the great weakness of Roman armies was lack of cavalry. The legionary infantry was superior to any that the world had yet seen, but without a good cavalry arm Roman armies were gravely handicapped. For this reason the Romans could never have been a match for the Macedonian armies of the fourth century'.[1]

It is apparent that Daniel's fourth empire is divided into two very distinct periods, one of strength and unity and one of weakness and division. The Greek empire was divided in exactly this way, whereas the Roman empire deteriorated very gradually and showed no such clear-cut division between strength and weakness, unity and division. The idea that the Roman empire still exists through the various countries which were once part of it (so fulfilling the prophecy of the feet of iron and clay) seems distinctly forced. These countries may certainly owe a great deal to the Romans, but this is not the same thing as being part of an existing Roman empire. They are certainly also disunited and of unequal strength, but, unlike the Greek empire, they provide no satisfactory and clear-cut explanation of the words, 'As you saw the iron mixed with miry clay, so they will mix with one another in marriage, but they will not hold together, just as iron does not mix with clay'.

In conclusion, therefore, the Greek empire perfectly fulfils every detail of the prophecy concerning the fourth kingdom, whereas the Roman empire falls short of the description in several respects.

Why separate Media and Persia?

It may have occurred to some readers to ask, 'Why does the book of Daniel complicate the issue by separating the Medes and Persians in chapters 2 and 7?'. Why could there not have been three kingdoms (Babylon, Medo-Persia and Greece) instead of four? It was not because the author had a mistaken view of history. There must be some good reason why God chose the four-kingdom sequence — and the following extract from an article by J. E. Goldingay[2] may well provide the answer we are looking for:

1. *A History of Warfare*, by B. L. Montgomery (Collins, 1968).
2. *Themelios*, January 1977.

'The four empire scheme resembles a pattern which appears in Greek, Latin and Persian writings, whereby four successive ages are symbolised by metals of diminishing strength or value, as in Daniel 2; the oldest certain occurrence of this symbolism comes in the eighth century Greek poet Hesiod (*Works and Days,* 106–201). These parallels suggest that Daniel's fourfold scheme pictures post-exilic history according to a common pattern. Probably it is more than merely a literary device; it makes a polemical point, like the use of near-Eastern mythological motifs elsewhere in the Old Testament. It expresses the conviction that Yahweh is the God who is really putting his will into effect in history. He is in control even of the degeneration which men can observe. Daniel applies the common image to the period of history with which he was concerned. This began with the Babylonians and ended with the Greeks, who thus have to be the first and last members of the scheme. What about the intervening material? Dr. Gurney suggests that this fits quite happily in between since a period of Median ascendancy occurred in between that of the Babylonians and of the Persians. But even if one has to grant that the material has to be squeezed (or rather stretched) to fit the scheme, this does not entail finding Daniel confused over post-exilic history. If he stretches a point over a period of history that is not in itself his main concern, this is because he is using an illustration which cannot be modified (otherwise, the point of using it disappears).'

The separation of Media and Persia in chapters 2 and 7 may appear to complicate things slightly; but it is done for a special purpose and involves no historical inaccuracies. We have shown that the descriptions of the four kingdoms tally exactly with Babylon, Media, Persia and Greece. We shall see in the following chapter that the vision of the four beasts continues the idea of the 'four kingdoms'; and it confirms what we should have deduced already — namely, that the four kingdoms are Babylon, Media, Persia and Greece. This still leaves us with the question, 'Why did God choose Greece to be the fourth kingdom and not Rome?' — but this will be dealt with in a later chapter.

The stone

Daniel goes on to say,

> '*As you looked, a stone was cut out by no human hand,*
> *and it smote the image on its feet of iron and clay, and*
> *broke them in pieces; then the iron, the clay, the bronze,*
> *the silver, and the gold, all together were broken in pieces,*
> *and became like the chaff of the summer threshing floors;*
> *and the wind carried them away, so that not a trace of*
> *them could be found. But the stone that struck the image*
> *became a great mountain and filled the whole earth.*'
> *(Daniel 2:34, 35)*

The interpretation is as follows:

> '*And in the days of those kings the God of heaven will set*
> *up a kingdom which shall never be destroyed, nor shall its*
> *sovereignty be left to another people. It shall break in*
> *pieces all these kingdoms and bring them to an end, and it*
> *shall stand for ever; just as you saw that a stone was cut*
> *from a mountain by no human hand, and that it broke in*
> *pieces the iron, the bronze, the clay, the silver, and the*
> *gold. A great God has made known to the king what shall*
> *be hereafter. The dream is certain, and its interpretation*
> *sure.*' *(Daniel 2:44, 45)*

A definite sequence of events is described here. A stone is
miraculously, by no human agency, cut out of a mountain. It
firstly smites the image upon its feet of iron and clay and
breaks them. After this the whole image is broken up together.
Finally, the stone becomes a great mountain filling the whole
earth. It is possible that the stone began to grow into a
mountain while it was still in the process of breaking up the
image; but to the author, the wording suggests rather that the
image was completely broken up *before* the stone began to
grow.

The radical critic, continuing to exclude all thought of the
miraculous, assumes here that his second century author is
predicting, hopefully but inaccurately, that God would destroy
Antiochus Epiphanes and the Greek empire and then immediately afterwards establish a world-wide kingdom of Heaven.
The possibility that this prophecy specifically predicts the

coming of Jesus Christ is dismissed as being incompatible with
rational thought. The prophecy is a noble idea, yes! A pious
hope, yes! But a genuine prediction, directly inspired by God,
which was actually fulfilled, no!

We shall see that this attitude is completely unjustified.
We shall see that the prophecy *has* been fulfilled in a most
wonderful way — just as we have seen that the description of
the four kingdoms is an *accurate* description of Babylon,
Media, Persia and Greece.

Let us leave aside, for a moment, the question of the
stone's identity, and try to interpret the break-up of the image.
The stone struck the image on its feet of iron and clay — the
feet which represent the decadent Greek empire. How was the
Greek empire actually destroyed? One very important thing
to note is that it was a gradual process — it did not happen
all at once. Macedon was defeated by Rome in 168 B.C. and
Israel broke free of Syria soon afterwards (both events taking
place during the reign of Antiochus Epiphanes). In 65 B.C.
Rome annexed Syria and in 27 B.C. she completed the process
by making Egypt a province of the Roman empire. (Macedon,
Syria and Egypt were the three main kingdoms into which the
Greek empire was divided.) The Parthians took over the eastern
part of the Empire.

How, then, are we to interpret the break-up of the image?
Note that in this vision (unlike that of chapter 7) the four
kingdoms are combined together in *a single structure*. And
this structure was probably the image of *a man*. The image
seems to be a symbol of man's power. But it may be more than
this. Illogical though it seems at first sight, it may also be a
symbol of the Greek empire. In a sense *the Greek empire was
a combination of all four kingdoms,* because it succeeded
Babylon, Media and Persia and absorbed all three of them into
its own structure. The four metals *individually* symbolise
Babylon, Media, Persia and Greece; but the image *as a whole*
symbolises both human political power and also the Greek
empire. The Greek empire assumes tremendous importance in
the book of Daniel, and is very much a symbol of man's
power — man in opposition to God.

We suggest, therefore, that the breaking of the image's feet
represents the beginning of the Greek empire's break-up (dur-

ing the reign of Antiochus Epiphanes), and the destruction of
the rest of the image represents the subsequent break-up of
the whole Greek empire (ending in 27 B.C.).

This interpretation is supported very strongly by certain
other parts of Daniel. In the vision of chapter 7 we are told
that the fourth beast was killed, *and then its body was destroyed.* This corresponds to the breaking of the image's feet
(the whole image must have crashed to the ground at this
point), followed by the destruction of the rest of its body.
In 8:25 we are specifically told that Antiochus was destroyed
by God, *and the wording of that verse is very closely related
to the wording of 2:34* (the verse which describes how the
stone broke the image's feet). We shall see that the destruction of Antiochus is also very closely associated with the
death of the fourth beast (7:11). And in 11:40–45 (a section
which follows a description of Antiochus Epiphanes and precedes a description of the kingdom of Heaven), we are given
a detailed description of the annexation of Syria and Egypt
by Rome. This corresponds to the break-up of the image's
body and the destruction of the body of the fourth beast. We
shall deal with all these points in much greater detail when
we come to the appropriate chapters; but we mention them
here to give some indication of how everything fits together.

We now come to the interpretation of 'the stone'. Jesus
Christ, who claimed to be the Messiah and the Son of God (and
proved it by rising from the dead), was born in about 6 B.C.,
*almost immediately after the final destruction of the Greek
empire.* From the very beginning of His public ministry He
began to preach, 'The time is fulfilled, and the kingdom of
God is at hand' (Mark 1:14). Furthermore He almost certainly
identified Himself as 'the stone' of Daniel 2.

> 'What then is this that is written: "The very stone which
> the builders rejected has become the head of the corner"?
> Every one who falls on that stone will be broken to pieces;
> but when it falls on any one it will crush him.' (Luke 20:
> 17, 18)

In this saying Jesus brings together three Old Testament symbols. Namely, the stone which became the head of the corner
(Psalm 118:22), the stone of stumbling (Isaiah 8:14, 15) and

the stone of Daniel 2:34, 35. He had just related the parable
of the vineyard, in which the tenants rejected and killed the
owner's son; and it is clear that He was identifying the rejected 'stone' with the rejected 'son'.

But Daniel 2:44, 45 also identifies this stone with a kingdom set up by God. It seems, therefore, to symbolise both
Christ Himself and also His kingdom, the Messianic kingdom
of Heaven. Another way of putting it is to say that it symbolises the rule and authority of Christ. As for the mountain
out of which the stone was cut, this probably refers to God
Himself.

There can be no shadow of doubt that as far as the New
Testament is concerned, God's kingdom was set up by Christ
some two thousand years ago. Jesus taught, 'The time is
fulfilled, and the kingdom of God is at hand' (Mark 1:15),
'The law and the prophets were until John; since then the
good news of the kingdom of God is preached' (Luke 16:16),
'The kingdom of God has come upon you' (Matthew 12:28),
'The kingdom of God is in the midst of you' (Luke 17:21).
Moreover He clearly taught, 'My kingship is not of this
world' (John 18:36). Christ's parable of the kingdom resem-
bling a mustard seed (Matthew 13:31, 32) is very similar to
the picture of the stone growing into a mountain.

It is said that a fatal objection to the Babylon-Media-
Persia-Greece interpretation is the statement that the heavenly
kingdom will be set up *in the days of* those kings' (Daniel
2:44), whereas Christ established His kingdom *after* the destruction of Greece. Note, however, that *the stone* (symbolising Christ) first destroys the fourth kingdom and *after* that
it grows into a mountain. The vision of Daniel 7 also clearly
indicates that Christ and the saints receive the Messianic
kingdom *after* the destruction of the fourth kingdom. There
is no problem here if we realise that *the fourth kingdom is
destroyed by the pre-incarnate Christ.* Christ can be said to
have set up His kingdom in the days of the Greek kings, in
that the process of setting up the kingdom included the destruction of the Greek empire. This is consistent with the
vision of Daniel 7, where the destruction of Antiochus and
the Greek empire is depicted as being the first step in the
process of setting up the kingdom of Heaven. Christ therefore

started the process of setting up His kingdom in the days of the Greek empire, but He continued the process after the empire had been destroyed.

When it was suggested above that the fourth kingdom was destroyed by the pre-incarnate Christ, some readers probably raised their eyebrows (metaphorically, if not literally!); so let us add a word of clarification before continuing. We shall see in the next chapter that the fourth beast of Daniel 7 symbolises the empire of Alexander and, after his death, the *Syrian* part of the Greek empire. We shall see that the beast's 'little horn' symbolises Antiochus Epiphanes, king of Syria. We shall also see that 8:25 clearly indicates that Antiochus was destroyed *by God,* and we shall see that the wording of that verse links it with 2:34 (which describes how the stone struck the image on its feet of iron and clay). These considerations make it likely that the feet of the image primarily, but not exclusively, symbolise the *Syrian* part of the Greek empire. As we shall see, there is no difficulty in understanding how God was responsible for the destruction of that empire. In one sense, of course, God is responsible for the destruction of all world powers; but we shall see that the Syrian Greek empire comes into a special category of its own. That empire deliberately tried to stamp out Judaism and it was the faithful worshippers of the one true God, motivated by religious zeal, who rose up against their Greek masters and defeated them again and again. In any case, as we have said, the book of Daniel itself clearly indicates in 8:25 that Antiochus, who was at the head of the Syrian Greek empire, was struck down by God Himself. Furthermore, the language employed links that verse with 2:34. We shall see later that it is possible to go even further and to deduce from 8:25 that it was *Christ* who destroyed Antiochus and the Greek empire.

We were saying that Christ began the process of setting up the kingdom of Heaven by destroying Antiochus and the Greek empire. Now some interpreters say that the process of setting up the kingdom did not *begin* with the destruction of the fourth kingdom. They say that the kingdom was first set up by Christ in the days of the Roman empire, but at the end of this age He will destroy the Roman empire (weakened and divided since the 5th century A.D.) and it is then, at the time of the second advent, that the stone will become a mountain. Obviously it would be fatal to this interpretation if it could be shown that the stone has *already* become (or is becoming) a mountain — and has been one since the time of the first advent. It would be fatal because the stone only begins to grow *after the destruction of the divided and weakened fourth empire*. The Roman empire simply *cannot* fit this picture of the fourth empire if the stone began to grow at the time of the first advent. The Roman empire was still expanding in the time of Christ, and it reached its greatest extent more than a century after His birth (during the reign of Trajan, 98—117 A.D.). When the western part of the empire eventually collapsed, over four centuries had passed since His birth. At this time the church had already grown into a large and powerful organisation. Moreover, these interpreters tell us that the Roman empire has not even been destroyed yet — they say it has been in its 'divided and weakened' state since the 5th century A.D.

Now there is, in fact, every reason to believe that the stone *has* already begun to grow into a mountain. Christ's parable of the mustard seed has already been mentioned. An even closer parallel is that of the stone which became the head of the corner. This stone was made the foundation stone of a great building which is even now in the process of being built up (Luke 20:17, 18; Acts 4:10, 11; Ephesians 2:19, 20; I Peter 2:3—5). This would indicate that the mountain is at least already growing. But in addition to this there are many passages which indicate that Christ's kingdom is, in fact, already filling the whole earth and has been doing so since the time of the first advent, long before even the division of the Roman empire. See, for example, Matthew 28:18; Ephesians 1:20—22; I Corinthians 15:24—28. These and other examples will be quoted in full in the following chapter.

In a certain restricted sense, the kingdom consists only of the true church of Christ (John 3:3; Matthew 18:3). In this sense the kingdom is still growing. But there seems to be another, wider sense in which the kingdom consists of Christ's universal rule in heaven and on earth. In this sense, the kingdom has filled the whole earth since the time of the first advent.

If, then, we take it that the stone has already at least begun to grow into the mountain, Rome is ruled out as the fourth
empire. The vision represents the kingdom of Heaven as
beginning to grow only *after Christ has destroyed the divided
and weakened fourth empire.* The Greek empire fits this
picture perfectly — shortly after the pre-incarnate Christ had
finally destroyed it, He entered this world to complete the
process of setting up His kingdom and it has been growing ever
since. More than this, He has possessed all authority in
heaven and on earth *since the time of the first advent.*

The image was a top-heavy structure with a weak and un-
stable foundation. The kingdom founded by Christ was a
massive, immovable mountain. What a contrast! Such is the
contrast between the best and most powerful of man's kingdoms and the kingdom of Christ.

It should be clear by now that the vision of Daniel 2 has
been perfectly fulfilled in every detail. The negative attitude
taken by critical scholars is completely unjustified. God *did*
destroy the image and He *has* set up His kingdom, precisely
as predicted.

The question of which advent

Now many conservative interpreters assume that Christ's
reference to the stone (Luke 20:18) shows that in His day
this part of Nebuchadnezzar's dream had yet to be fulfilled.
But this is not necessarily so at all. Christ was obviously
identifying Himself with the stone, but He was employing a
past event as an illustration or 'type' of a future event. Christ
was not speaking of the event in Daniel (except in a secondary
sense), because there the stone destroys only the four kingdoms, whereas Christ gives a much wider application, saying,
'when it falls on any one'. Christ was speaking of the judgment which is eventually to fall upon *all* His enemies (and
particularly the judgment which was then shortly to fall upon
the Jews). The destruction of the image *typifies* his future
destruction of all world powers.

A few paragraphs back we noted that some conservative
interpreters maintain that the heavenly kingdom of Nebuchadnezzar's vision did not *begin* with the destruction of the

fourth empire. It can hardly be denied, however, that we do get the distinct impression that the heavenly kingdom began by destroying the fourth empire. Perhaps it is no more than an impression in this vision; but in the next vision it is stated quite clearly. The latter vision plainly indicates that the fourth empire was utterly destroyed before the saints possessed the kingdom.

At this point these interpreters will hasten to tell us that the kingdom of chapter 7 is not quite the same thing as the kingdom of chapter 2. The latter kingdom was established by Christ at the time of the first advent, whereas chapter 7 only describes a kingdom which will be established after the second advent. The stone, they will tell us, represents the kingdom Christ established some two thousand years ago. At the time of the second advent it will destroy the fourth empire and become a world-dominating power, as represented by its growth into the mountain — and it is *this* stage of the kingdom which is pictured in chapter 7.

According to this theory, the description of the kingdom in chapter 2 is largely a description of Christ's kingdom during and after the second advent. Little is said about the kingdom *already* established by Christ apart from the statement that it was founded in the days of the four empires (2:44). All the 'action' is reserved for the time of the second advent. Even more drastically, chapter 7 has *nothing whatever* to say about the present kingdom — it passes over it in complete silence and concentrates entirely on a kingdom to be founded after the second advent.

Superficially, all this may look quite reasonable. But in fact the perspective is all wrong. One of the gravest weaknesses of the orthodox and dispensationalist theories is the lack of attention paid to the kingdom which Christ established at the time of His first advent. They give it a little attention in the first vision, but completely ignore it in the second. We have to bear in mind that these visions were seen at a time when the arrival of the Messiah and His kingdom was the great event to come. The New Testament repeatedly declares that Christ's *first advent* was what all the prophets had been talking about. In our own times the second advent is the great event to come; but in Old Testament times it was the first advent that filled the prophetic horizon. We can expect to find a good deal about the second advent in the book of Revelation; but on the authority of the New Testament itself, we should expect to find far more about the first advent in the book of Daniel.

'And all the prophets who have spoken, from Samuel and those who came afterwards, also proclaimed *these days.*' (Acts 3:24)

'Behold, we are going up to Jerusalem, and everything that is written of the Son of man by the prophets will be accomplished . . .' (Luke 18:31)

'For these men are not drunk, as you suppose . . . but this is what was spoken by the prophet Joel: "And in *the last days* it shall be, God declares, that I will pour out my Spirit upon all flesh . . ." ' (Acts 2:15–17)

'In many and various ways God spoke of old to our fathers by the prophets; but in *these last days* he has spoken to us by a Son.' (Hebrews 1:1, 2)

'. . . since the foundation of the world. But as it is, he has appeared once for all at *the end of the age* to put away sin by the sacrifice of himself.' (Hebrews 9:26)

'He was destined before the foundation of the world but was made manifest at *the end of the times* for your sake.' (I Peter 1:20)

Despite this, Daniel's prophecies undoubtedly do contain much that is relevant to the second advent. The way in which certain past events can typify things yet to come has already been mentioned. In addition, we are told that the heavenly kingdom will fill the whole earth and have absolute dominion (chapter 7). Clearly this prophecy will find its most complete fulfilment some time in the future – and yet it is all part of the kingdom which Christ established some two thousand years ago.

Nebuchadnezzar saw a stone which destroyed an image and became a great mountain filling the whole earth. These few words describe the history of Christ's kingdom – a history which is unfolding over a period of many centuries. When we look at a range of mountains from a distance, the individual mountains appear very close together. It is only when we come close that we see the great distances between them. The kingdom which Daniel saw from a distance was foreshortened (as described in our introduction) in the same way. He saw *when* the kingdom was to be established and that it was to fill the whole earth; but there is much that he was not told. He was not told that many centuries were to elapse between the founding of the kingdom and the time when it would, in every sense of the phrase, 'fill the whole earth'. This was something which became apparent only after the time of Christ — although Christ Himself predicted it clearly enough.

A similar technique is used in Zechariah 9:9, 10. These verses clearly refer to Christ's triumphant entry into Jerusalem at the time of His first advent (Matthew 21:1—11), and yet at the same time they speak of His universal dominion. *In the same way* Daniel speaks of Christ's first advent and universal dominion, but gives no indication of the long period of time involved.

Now the author realises that his reasoning so far will not convince every reader. For example, there are some who reject the idea of a revived or continuing Roman empire and accept that the stone began to grow at the time of the first advent, but they still manage to believe that Rome was the fourth kingdom. They do this by maintaining that verses 34, 35, 44 and 45 could describe a gradual break-up of the image as the stone grows into a mountain. In other words, the fourth kingdom gradually disintegrated at the same time that the kingdom of Heaven was growing. The author agrees that it is possible to maintain that the stone began to grow into a mountain immediately after striking the fourth kingdom, while it was still in the process of breaking up the image; but it is difficult to maintain that the stone began to grow *before* it struck the fourth kingdom. Yet this is exactly what we have to believe if we regard Rome as the fourth kingdom and the stone as beginning to grow at the time of the first advent.

Let the reader consider, for a moment, the fact that the Roman empire reached its greatest extent during the reign of Trajan in the second century A.D., many years after the time of Christ. Trajan was the second of the 'five good emperors', whose era can be regarded as the 'golden age' of the Roman empire. At this time Rome was at the zenith of its power. It was powerful, secure, prosperous and at peace within its own borders — more so than at any other time in its history. By this time Christianity had spread to most if not all parts of the Roman empire and far beyond. When the western empire eventually broke up, some four hundred years had passed since the time of Christ. *Let it be clearly understood that the Roman empire did not begin to break up until long after the kingdom of Heaven began to grow.*

We repeat that if the growth of the stone into a mountain represents the spread of Christianity and the growth of the church (not to mention Christ's universal rule in heaven and on earth), it cannot be said that Rome fulfils the picture of the fourth kingdom.

We shall now go on to consider the vision of chapter 7. We shall see that it provides very strong support for our interpretation, because it clearly indicates that the fourth empire was utterly destroyed before Christ and the saints received the kingdom at the time of the first advent.

CHAPTER THREE

The Four Beasts

We find the vision of the four beasts in the seventh chapter of Daniel. This time it is Daniel himself who dreams the dream. In awe-inspiring language he describes the beasts rising out of the 'sea' of humanity.[1]

> 'In the first year of Belshazzar king of Babylon, Daniel had a dream and visions of his head as he lay in his bed. Then he wrote down the dream, and told the sum of the matter. Daniel said, " I saw in my vision by night, and behold, the four winds of heaven were stirring up the great sea. And four great beasts came up out of the sea, different from one another." ' (Daniel 7:1–3)

The first beast

> 'The first was like a lion and had eagles' wings. Then as I looked its wings were plucked off, and it was lifted up from the ground and made to stand upon two feet like a man; and the mind of a man was given to it.' (Daniel 7:4)

The winged lion is familiar in Babylonian art. The eagle was a symbol of swiftness and the lion one of strength and nobility (II Samuel 1:23). The eagle was the king of birds, and the lion the king of beasts. They correspond to the image's head of gold, the metal which was regarded as the noblest and most valuable of all metals. Almost all are agreed that this beast represents Babylon and that the change which comes upon it probably symbolises Nebuchadnezzar's madness and subsequent restoration (Daniel 4). Note that again Babylon *in the time of Nebuchadnezzar* is strongly indicated. The Bible repeatedly describes Nebuchadnezzar and the Chaldeans of his

1. Cf. Revelations 13:1; 17:3; 15.

time as being like both an eagle[2] and a lion.[3] These creatures
were used to convey a picture of Nebuchadnezzar coming from
afar against the Jews and their neighbours, and carrying them
off as captives to Babylon. The book of Daniel always
associates the glory and magnificence of Babylon with
Nebuchadnezzar, and it emphasises his greatness again and
again.[4]

It is a historical fact that Nebuchadnezzar was largely
responsible for the glory of the neo-Babylonian empire. He
came to the throne when his father died in 605 B.C., soon
after the final obliteration of Assyria — an event which
Nebuchadnezzar helped to bring about. During his long reign
of 43 years, Babylon was practically invincible. Moreover he
lavished immense wealth and architectural skill on his capital
city, making it world-famous for its magnificence and strength.
Nebuchadnezzar was both a great soldier and a great builder.
After his death, however, a series of relatively weak kings
followed each other in rapid succession and Babylon's power
declined. She was still a power, but whereas she formerly had
the edge on her great rival, Media, the position was now reversed.

The second beast

*'And behold, another beast, a second one, like a bear. It
was raised up on one side; it had three ribs in its mouth
between its teeth; and it was told, "Arise, devour much
flesh".' (Daniel 7:5)*

Although the bear is not so swift as the lion, it was
equally feared owing to its great strength and the unpredict-
ability of its actions. The lion and bear are mentioned together
a number of times in Scripture,[5] and both were clearly
objects of special fear and respect. In a similar way the rival

2.   Deuteronomy 28:49—53 (cf. II Kings 25:1—11); Jeremiah 49:19,
     22; Lamentations 4:19; Ezekiel 17:1—5, 11—14; Habakkuk 1:6—8.

3.   Isaiah 5:25—30; Jeremiah 4:6, 7, 13 (cf. 25:9, 38); 49:19, 22;
     50:17, 44.

4.   Daniel 2:37, 38; 4:22, 30, 36; 5:18, 19.

5.   I Samuel 17:34; Proverbs 28:15; Lamentations 3:10; Amos 5:19.

powers of Babylon and Media together commanded the nations' fear and respect. The bear is a comparatively slow-moving and clumsy creature; therefore this symbol applies better to the Median empire than to the Persian. The career of Cyrus the Persian was characterised by a succession of swift and brilliant victories, better symbolised by the next beast, which is a leopard.

We are told that the bear 'was raised up on one side'. This may mean that one side was higher than the other as it stood on all fours. Or it could mean that one forepaw was raised off the ground as if it were in the act of raising itself up into a standing position on its hindlegs. If the latter is what Daniel means, the figure could symbolise a nation rousing itself for conquest. The beast could be raising itself in response to the command 'Arise, devour much flesh'; but it is not ready yet. This is a good picture of Media, because although she began to *prepare* for Babylon's conquest, she never completed the task by herself. She did take part in the final destruction of Babylon, but only as the partner (and the inferior one at that) of Persia.

However, the main explanation of the bear's attitude is this. *Media's period of power was divided into two very different stages.* During the first stage she was the powerful head of a large empire — this is represented by the side of the bear which is raised up. During the second stage she was the somewhat inferior partner of Persia. Daniel is careful to emphasise (chapters 5, 6 and 8) that the Medes and Persians *ruled together as allies* for a number of years following Cyrus's victory over the Median king in 550 B.C. This part of Media's reign is represented by the lower side of the bear. During her partnership with Persia, she was still ruling the nations, but in a humbler capacity than before. Her partnership with Persia constituted the world's most powerful empire; but despite the exalted nature of her continued ruling of the nations, it was not as exalted as it had been before the rise of Persia.

We are told that three ribs were in the bear's mouth between its teeth, and that it was commanded, 'Arise, devour much flesh'. These points seem to have caused a certain amount of confusion among interpreters; but in actual fact they provide very strong evidence that the bear symbolises Media. It is generally agreed that the three ribs must represent three nations conquered by the bear, and that the bear is ordered to arise and make fresh conquests. However, the identities of the three nations have remained in doubt. The Bible itself provides the answer. In the book of Jeremiah we read the following words directed against Babylon:

> 'Set up a standard on the earth, blow the trumpet among the nations; prepare the nations for war against her, summon against her the kingdoms, Ararat, Minni, and Ashkenaz; appoint a marshal against her, bring up horses like bristling locusts. Prepare the nations for war against her, the kings of the Medes, with their governors and deputies, and every land under their dominion. The land trembles and writhes in pain, for the Lord's purposes against Babylon stand, to make the land of Babylon a desolation, without inhabitant.' (Jeremiah 51:27–29)

In this passage God stirs up four nations against Babylon. This reminds us that the bear with the three ribs was also stirred up — and probably against Babylon. Three of these nations were the small kingdoms of Ararat, Minni and Ashkenaz. They all lay to the North of Babylon and *all were within the Median empire*. The fourth nation was the Median empire itself. *The bear with the three ribs between its teeth is a perfect picture of the Median empire and the three small subject kingdoms of Ararat, Minni and Ashkenaz.* Note that *Media* is the principal nation stirred up against Babylon. In the eleventh verse of the same chapter of Jeremiah we read,

> 'The Lord has stirred up the spirit of the kings of the Medes, because his purpose concerning Babylon is to destroy it . . .'

In Isaiah 13:17 we read, concerning the Babylonians,

> 'Behold, I am stirring up the Medes against them . . .'

We can see, therefore, that the prophets repeatedly proclaimed *God would stir up the Medes against Babylon. This is the meaning of the command to arise and devour much flesh.*

In Isaiah 21:2 Media *and Elam* are ordered to besiege Babylon and in verse 9 the fall of Babylon is proclaimed (pro-

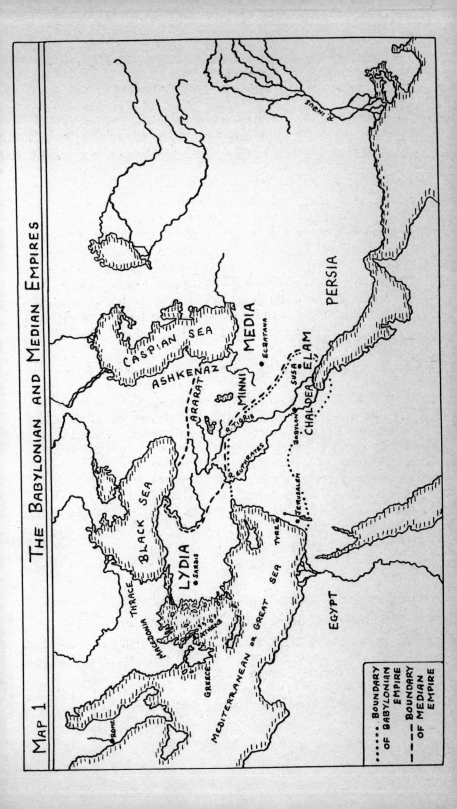

MAP 1   THE BABYLONIAN AND MEDIAN EMPIRES

······ BOUNDARY
OF BABYLONIAN
EMPIRE

—— — BOUNDARY
OF MEDIAN
EMPIRE

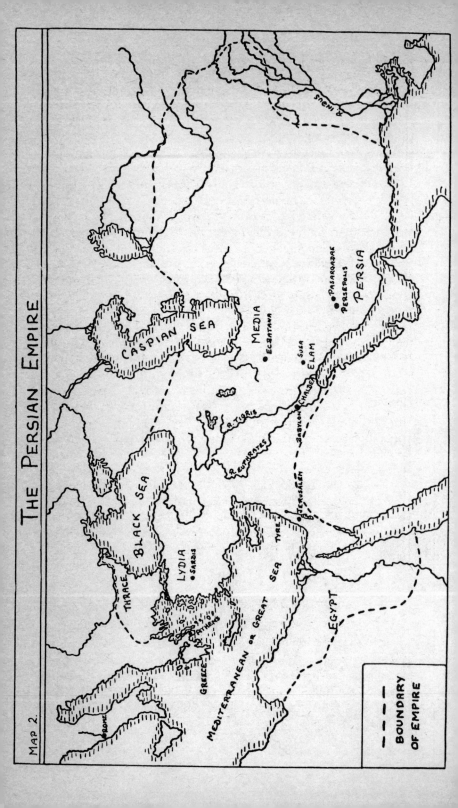

MAP 2.

THE PERSIAN EMPIRE

BOUNDARY
OF EMPIRE

phetically). By the time Media got round to actually besieging Babylon, it had become the inferior partner of Persia. The reference to Elam is explained by the fact that Anshan, the small Persian kingdom where Cyrus first came to power, was situated in the eastern part of ancient Elam. It is also relevant, perhaps, that Gobryas, the general who captured the city of Babylon, was the governor of Elam (i.e., the western, Babylonian part) before he deserted to Cyrus.

Thus the general picture we have is that Media became stronger than Babylon on the death of Nebuchadnezzar and *planned* to overcome her, being stirred up to this by God. But before Media was able to carry her plans into effect, she was joined and surpassed by Persia. Under the leadership of Cyrus the Persian, however, she was able to take part in the eventual overthrow of Babylon.

There is a significant omission from the prophecies concerning the stirring up of Media against Babylon. Ararat, Minni, Ashkenaz and Media were all near to Babylonia, being ranged round its northern and eastern borders. Persian-occupied eastern Elam was also on the border of Babylonia, being just to the South of Media. Since eastern Elam (i.e., Persia) was, like the three other small kingdoms, subject to Media, it might be expected that it also would have been 'stirred up' against Babylon during the time of the latter's decay and Media's ascendancy. The reason for its omission is the fact that Babylon and Persia arranged an alliance together against Media. This was the situation during Media's period of supreme power; but it was reversed when Cyrus overcame the Median king, because the combination of Persia and Media was now the principal threat to Babylon.

The third beast

'After this I looked, and lo, another, like the leopard, with four wings of a bird on its back; and the beast had four heads; and dominion was given to it.' (Daniel 7:6)

The swift and agile winged leopard contrasts vividly with the clumsy, lop-sided bear. Such was the contrast between the ponderous Median empire and the brilliant, swiftly-moving armies of Cyrus the Persian. The early kings that followed

Cyrus were not as brilliant as he, but they certainly moved much faster and more purposefully than the Medes.

Now the main characteristic of this third kingdom is, like that of the 'bronze' kingdom, one of widespread authority or 'dominion', which was the chief characteristic of Persia. This is shown by the four wings symbolising the four winds, one for each of the 'four corners of the earth'.[6] On a clay cylinder Cyrus, founder of the Persian empire, described himself as 'king of the four corners of the earth'. On another he said, 'Sin, the light of heaven . . . gave into my hands the four corners of the earth'.

There is a famous four-winged figure on the door-jamb of one of the entrances to Cyrus's palace at Pasargadae, in Persia. It bore his name, but possibly represented a protective genius. Besides the four wings on its back, the figure has what appear to be two horns protruding from its head. In Daniel 8 the Persian empire is represented as a two-horned ram, the horns symbolising the Median and Persian elements of that empire. There may be no connection, but it is interesting to imagine that through the centuries God may have preserved this lonely, silent monument as a guide to the meaning of Daniel's prophecy.

The beast had four heads. Now a head naturally suggests a king or some similar authority. In the eleventh chapter of Daniel we are specially told about *four kings of Persia*. The first is Cyrus and the fourth is Xerxes. This interpretation of the meaning of the four heads is eminently suitable, because Persia's main period of expansion and aggression only covered the reigns of these first four kings — Cyrus, Cambyses, Darius and Xerxes (Pseudo-Smerdis being merely a short-lived impostor). Between them, these four kings created the Persian empire in all its vast extent and wealth; and it was after the reign of Xerxes that the decline of the empire began. Xerxes' small gains in Greece were lost within a few months; but the empire reached the pinnacle of its power, wealth and size during his reign. Each one of these four kings had a part to play in the creation of this enormous empire. It was not the work of one man, and the four-headed beast is a perfect picture of this.

6.   See Psalm 104:3 and Zechariah 2:6 — 'the wings of the wind' and 'I have spread you abroad as the four winds of the heavens'.

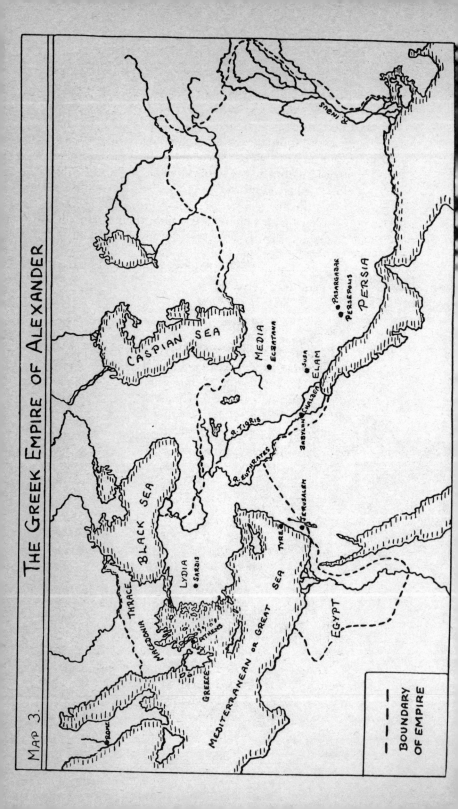

MAP 3.

THE GREEK EMPIRE OF ALEXANDER

BOUNDARY
OF EMPIRE

We can see therefore that whatever resemblance the beast might have to any other empire, it was fulfilled *in every respect* by the Persian empire. Let it again be pointed out that the only thing said about the beast's rule was the fact that it was to have *dominion* — which corresponds to the statement that the bronze kingdom was to 'rule over all the earth'. This was by far the most striking aspect of the Persian empire. It was several times the size of any previous empire. The Greek empire, on the other hand, was no larger than the Persian, and was probably in fact slightly smaller. Moreover the Persians maintained their vast empire for over two hundred years, whereas the Greek empire was broken up and reduced in size only nine years after its foundation.

The fourth beast

'*After this I saw in the night visions, and behold, a fourth beast, terrible and dreadful and exceedingly strong; and it had great iron teeth; it devoured and broke in pieces, and stamped the residue with its feet. It was different from all the beasts that were before it . . .* ' (Daniel 7:7)

'*Then I desired to know the truth concerning the fourth beast, which was different from all the rest, exceedingly terrible, with its teeth of iron and claws of bronze; and which devoured and broke in pieces, and stamped the residue with its feet . . .* ' (Daniel 7:19)

'*As for the fourth beast, there shall be a fourth kingdom on earth, which shall be different from all the kingdoms, and it shall devour the whole earth, and trample it down, and break it to pieces . . .* ' (Daniel 7:23)

The remarks made about the legs of iron in the first vision also apply to this fourth beast. It is not likened to any known animal. In strength, ferocity and probably speed it exceeded anything the Orient could imagine. From the distant West Alexander descended on the East like a thunderclap, shattering the armies of Earth's mightiest empire with a speed and thoroughness the world had never witnessed before. The verses quoted above convey very vividly the sense of terror which struck the East when the powerful city of Tyre fell to Alexander in 332 B.C. (see Ezekiel 26:15–21).

The fourth beast is said to be 'different' from the first three beasts. The western nation of Greece was a complete contrast to the oriental Babylonian, Median and Persian empires. Her culture was utterly alien and her method of fighting was also completely different, enabling her with small armies easily to defeat the vast but unwidlldy hosts of the East.

Rome, on the other hand, was in many respects very similar to Greece. She was a western power of the same racial stock and the same culture and her fighting methods were similarly efficient. In this respect, therefore, Greece fits the fourth beast much better than Rome.

We are told that the fourth kingdom treads down '*the whole earth*' and we are given the impression that it crushes the first three kingdoms (2:40; 7:7, 23). In the context of the book of Daniel, 'the whole earth' must surely include the area covered by the Babylonian, Median, Persian and Greek empires — an area which completely swamped the tiny land of Israel. In this respect Greece would appear to be far more suitable than Rome. It will be remembered that like the fourth kingdom, the third kingdom also rules over 'all the earth'. Now apart from some border areas, Greece took over the whole Persian empire, lock, stock and barrel — including Babylonia and Media. Thus the third and fourth kingdoms both rule over 'the whole earth'; and regarding this, we note that Greece ruled over almost the same vast area as Persia.

Rome, on the other hand, did not by any means tread down 'the whole earth' in this context. The Roman empire was essentially an empire of the West and Palestine lay right on its eastern border. All the land to the immediate east of Palestine (including Babylonia, Media and Persia) lay *outside the Roman empire.* Trajan did incorporate Armenia, Mesopotamia and Assyria (the names given to the new provinces) into the Roman empire for a very short period in the second century A.D.; but his successor Hadrian immediately abandoned them. Later emperors had to annex territory in the East at various times in efforts to find a satisfactory frontier, but the empire reached its greatest extent during the reign of Trajan — long after the coming of the kingdom of Heaven. Most of the Median empire and about half of the Persian and Greek empires were never at any time within the Roman empire. Media and Persia

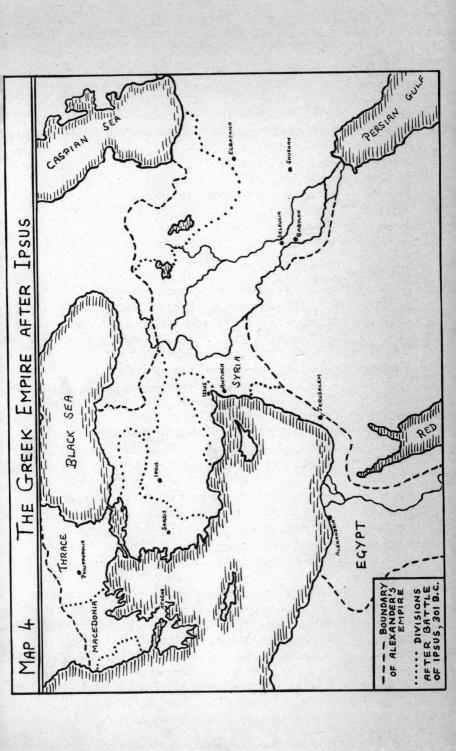

MAP 4   THE GREEK EMPIRE AFTER IPSUS

CASPIAN SEA

PERSIAN GULF

ECBATANA

SHUSHAN

SELEUCIA

BABYLON

BLACK SEA

ANTIOCH

SYRIA

ISSUS

JERUSALEM

RED

THRACE

PHILIPPOPOLIS

IPSUS

SARDIS

ATHENS

MACEDONIA

ALEXANDRIA

EGYPT

--- BOUNDARY
OF ALEXANDER'S
EMPIRE

..... DIVISIONS
AFTER BATTLE
OF IPSUS, 301 B.C.

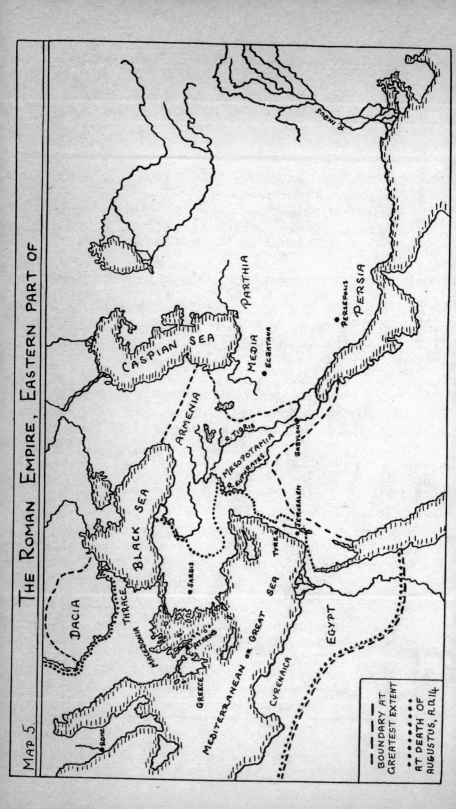

themselves were never within the empire. Thus *in this context* Rome cannot be said to have trodden down 'the whole earth'.

The horns of the fourth beast

'. . . and it had ten horns. I considered the horns, and behold, there came up among them another horn, a little one, before which three of the first horns were plucked up by the roots; and behold, in this horn were eyes like the eyes of a man, and a mouth speaking great things.' (Daniel 7:7, 8)

'. . . and concerning the ten horns that were on its head, and the other horn which came up and before which three of them fell, the horn which had eyes and a mouth that spoke great things, and which seemed greater than its fellows. As I looked, this horn made war with the saints, and prevailed over them.' (Daniel 7:20, 21)

'As for the ten horns, out of this kingdom ten kings shall arise, and another shall arise after them; he shall be different from the former ones, and shall put down three kings. He shall speak words against the Most High, and shall wear out the saints of the Most High, and shall think to change the times and the law; and they shall be given into his hand for a time, two times, and half a time.' (Daniel 7:24, 25)

The identities of the ten horns and the little horn have been the subject of much controversy. They probably occur during a second phase of the beast's rule and correspond to the image's feet of iron and clay. The number ten should be taken literally in view of the fact that the four horns of the he-goat (chapter 8) literally symbolise four kingdoms. Now the ten kings are *not* necessarily contemporaneous. Compare the image's four metals which all appeared together and yet were essentially consecutive — likewise the heads of the third beast and the one-sided raising of the second beast. If the horns collectively represent a second phase of the beast's rule, it is appropriate that they should appear together — even if they represent kings that are consecutive rather than contemporaneous.

A very reasonable and logical interpretation is that the first seven horns represent the seven Seleucid kings (the dynasty set up over the Syrian part of the empire after the death of Alexander and minutely described in Daniel 11) from Seleucus Nicator to Seleucus Philopater. Antiochus Epiphanes became king not long after the death of his brother Philopater, but his rise to power involved the disposal of three people. They were

1. *Demetrius,* son of Philopater and rightful heir to the throne, who was sent to Rome by his father as a hostage in return for Antiochus. He later returned to Syria and became its king after Antiochus had died, Antiochus having usurped the kingdom in his absence.

2. *Heliodorus,* the king's minister, who poisoned Seleucus Philopater when he saw that Demetrius, the heir, was out of the way and himself usurped the kingdom.

3. *Antiochus,* baby son of Philopator. Antiochus Epiphanes reigned with him (after Heliodorus had been disposed of) until the child was murdered after five years.

The manner in which Antiochus Epiphanes displaced these three kings is very aptly pictured by the little horn arising among three horns and plucking them up by the roots. There are many who feel that this interpretation is not entirely satisfactory, because Demetrius, Heliodorus and Antiochus were not 'kings' in quite the same sense as their seven predecessors. It is probable, however, that the tearing up of these three horns by the roots indicates the very fact that they did not attain the degree of kingship enjoyed by the first seven kings. Another objection is that Heliodorus was not a Seleucid by descent. This does not matter at all, since the vision merely indicates that the ten kings were of Greek origin.

However, it is true that there is some uncertainty about the identity of these last three kings. This uncertainty has enabled orthodox interpreters to maintain that the three horns cannot be identified and that the fourth beast therefore has nothing to do with Greece. Surely they are dismissing the matter too lightly. The solution outlined above is perfectly adequate in spite of the objections raised against it.

The fact that some interpreters prefer other solutions does not negate the fact that at least one good solution does exist. It is a historical fact that there were *seven* Seleucid kings before Antiochus Epiphanes appeared on the scene, and that *three* more individuals stood in his path to the throne. Each of these three could in some way lay claim to the description of 'king'. This combination of circumstances was very distinctive and possibly even unique. It is really too much to say that it is all a pure coincidence, especially when one takes into account the fact that the Greek empire is one of the two chief candidates for identification with the beast — also the fact that the Greek empire, the majority of the ten kings and Antiochus Epiphanes are all minutely described in chapters 8 and 11.

We may now consider the little horn. It need hardly be said that the description of this horn is a perfect description of Antiochus Epiphanes. It is at first said to be 'little', but later we are told that it is 'greater' than its fellows. In other words, from small beginnings it becomes great. Antiochus started his career as the younger brother of Seleucus Philopator, with no right to the throne, a hostage in Rome. From these small beginnings he became, as we are told in Daniel 8:9, 'exceedingly great'. The eyes refer perhaps to his cunning and vigilance. The mouth speaking great things, words against the Most High, refers to his boastful and blasphemous opposition to the God of Israel. He affected the title of *Theos Epiphanes,* 'God Manifest', as he looked on himself as an incarnate manifestation of Olympian Zeus.

We are told that the little horn makes war with the saints and prevails against them and thinks to change the times and the law. Antiochus savagely persecuted the faithful of Israel and abolished and sought to stamp out Judaism. He did all in his power to put down the temple ritual, the sacred scriptures, the Sabbath and other festival days, the food laws and the rite of circumcision.

We are told that the times and the law are 'given into its (the little horn's) hand till a time, and times, and a division of a time' (see A.V. and Young's Literal Translation — 'half' in the R.S.V. is a translation of *pelag* which merely indicates a division, and does not necessarily mean a half) — that is, 'three times and a fraction of a time'. Revelation 12 indicates that this 'time' is a year of 360 days.[7] Thus certain ordinances are given into the hand of the little horn for three years plus part of a year. In 167 B.C.[8] Antiochus ordered the daily sacrifice and other Jewish observances to cease. They came to an end probably around the middle of that year, though this could have occurred more towards the end of the year. Later, in December (15th Kislev), he erected an altar to Olympian Zeus in the temple court. Exactly three years after the commencement of the pagan sacrifices (25th Kislev, 164 B.C.), the victorious Jews recommenced the daily sacrifice, having removed the false high priest installed by Antiochus. Thus 'the times and the law' were indeed given into the hand of Antiochus for three years plus part of a year. We shall be seeing, when we come to Daniel 12, that this was probably a period of 1290 days.

The destruction of the fourth beast and the rise of the kingdom of Heaven

'*As I looked, thrones were placed and one that was ancient of days took his seat; his raiment was white as snow, and the hair of his head like pure wool; his throne was fiery flames, its wheels were burning fire. A stream of fire issued and came forth from before him; a thousand thousands served him, and ten thousand times ten thousand stood before him; the court sat in judgment, and the books were opened. I looked then because of the sound of the great words which the horn was speaking. And as I looked, the beast was slain, and its body destroyed and given over to be burned with fire. As for the rest of the beasts, their dominion was taken away, but their lives were prolonged for a season and a time.*' (Daniel 7:9—12)

'*I saw in the night visions, and behold, with the clouds of heaven there came one like a son of man, and he came to*

---

7. In Revelation 12 a period of 1260 days is defined as being three and a half 'times' (vv. 6, 14) — the Greek word *hemisu* definitely meaning 'half' in that instance.

8. 167 or 168 B.C. There is an uncertainty of one year with all dates in the Seleucid era; but this does not affect the interpretation of Daniel's prophecies.

the Ancient of Days and was presented before him. And to him was given dominion and glory and kingdom, that all peoples, nations, and languages should serve him; his dominion is an everlasting dominion, which shall not pass away, and his kingdom one that shall not be destroyed.' (Daniel 7:13, 14)

Daniel's informant explains,

'These four great beasts are four kings who shall arise out of the earth. But the saints of the Most High shall receive the kingdom, and possess the kingdom for ever, for ever and ever.' (Daniel 7:17, 18)

Daniel states further that the little horn

'. . . made war with the saints, and prevailed over them, until the Ancient of Days came, and judgment was given for the saints of the Most High, and the time came when the saints received the kingdom.' (Daniel 7:21, 22)

Daniel's informant explains further,

'But the court shall sit in judgment, and his dominion shall be taken away, to be consumed and destroyed to the end. And the kingdom and the dominion and the greatness of the kingdoms under the whole heaven shall be given to the people of the saints of the Most High; their kingdom shall be an everlasting kingdom, and all dominions shall serve and obey them.' (Daniel 7:26, 27)

These passages describe the destruction of the fourth beast and the rise of the kingdom of Heaven. Now there are three very definite stages in this drama. Moreover, the language precludes the possibility of their occurring instantaneously — they cover a period of time.

Stage 1. The fourth beast and the little horn are judged by the Ancient of Days and the saints are vindicated. Therefore the beast and the little horn are slain — the saints perhaps being instrumental in the execution of judgment.

Stage 2. The body of the fourth beast is then destroyed. Although the other three kingdoms have their authority taken from them, they are not yet destroyed.

Stage 3. The time then comes that 'one like a son of man' is brought before the Ancient of Days and is given dominion and glory and an everlasting kingdom.

We should now try to identify the new characters in the vision. The 'Ancient of Days' is God Himself — that is, God the Father; and a 'saint' is a true and faithful servant of God. The 'one like a son of man' is unquestionably Jesus Christ Himself, although he is perhaps to some extent identified with the saints (vv.18, 27).[9] Jesus constantly referred to Himself as the 'Son of man' in terms which were obviously connected with Daniel 7:13. For example, He said to the High Priest, 'Hereafter you will see the Son of man seated at the right hand of Power, and coming on the clouds of heaven' (Matthew 26:64).

It is likewise just as unquestionable that He received His kingdom when He ascended up to Heaven after His work on earth was finished. The parable of a nobleman going into a far country to receive for himself a kingdom was a parable of this event and the return of the nobleman pictures the second advent (Luke 19:12—27).

'Truly, I say to you, there are some standing here who will not taste death before they see the Son of man coming in his kingdom.' (Matthew 16:28; see also Matthew 10:23)

'But I tell you, hereafter you will see the Son of man seated at the right hand of Power, and coming on the clouds of heaven.' (Matthew 26:64)

'But from now on the Son of man shall be seated at the right hand of the power of God.' (Luke 22:69)

'All authority in heaven and on earth has been given to me.' (Matthew 28:18)

'Behold, I see the heavens opened, and the Son of man standing at the right hand of God.' (Acts 7:56)

'. . . which he accomplished in Christ when he raised him from the dead and made him sit at his right hand in the

9. See *Daniel's Vision of the Son of Man*, by E. J. Young, (Tyndale Press, 1958). Young suggests that the saints receive the kingdom *from the Son of Man*. See also Ephesians 1:18 — 2:6; Revelation 5:9–13. Much has been written on this subject, but we cannot go into all the details here. For our purpose the important question is, how did *Jesus* interpret the vision?

heavenly places, far above all rule and authority and power and dominion, and above every name that is named, not only in this age but also in that which is to come; and he has put all things under his feet . . .' (Ephesians 1:20—22)

'When he had made purification for sins, he sat down at the right hand of the Majesty on high . . .' (Hebrews 1:3)

'. . . Jesus Christ, who has gone into heaven and is at the right hand of God, with angels, authorities, and powers subject to him.' (I Peter 3:21, 22)

'. . . she brought forth a male child, one who is to rule all the nations with a rod of iron, but her child was caught up to God and to his throne . . .' (Revelation 12:5)

'. . . Jesus Christ . . . the ruler of kings on earth.' (Revelation 1:5)

'He who conquers, I will grant him to sit with me on my throne, as I myself conquered and sat down with my Father on his throne.' (Revelation 3:21)

'. . . thou wast slain, and didst purchase unto God with thy blood men of every tribe, and tongue, and people, and nation, and madest them to be unto our God a kingdom and priests; and they reign upon the earth . . . Worthy is the Lamb that hath been slain to receive the power, and riches, and wisdom, and might, and honour, and glory, and blessing . . . Unto him that sitteth on the throne, and unto the Lamb, be the blessing, and the honour, and the glory, and the dominion, for ever and ever.' (Revelation 5:9—13, R.V.)

'But in fact Christ has been raised from the dead . . . Christ the first fruits, then at his coming those who belong to Christ. Then comes the end, when he delivers the kingdom to God the Father after destroying every rule and every authority and power. For he must reign until he has put all his enemies under his feet. The last enemy to be destroyed is death. "For God has put all things in subjection under his feet." . . . When all things are subjected to him, then the Son himself will also be subjected to him who put all things under him, that God may be everything to every one.' (I Corinthians 15:20—28)

These wonderful passages clearly indicate that Christ 're-ceived the kingdom' at the time of His resurrection and ascension. This rules out the possibility of the fourth kingdom being Rome, because Daniel plainly shows that the fourth kingdom and the little horn would first be completely des-troyed and *after that* the Son of man would receive His kingdom.

Having seen how this part of the vision does *not* apply to the destruction of the Roman empire, let us see how it *does* apply to the destruction of the Greek empire. But before we do this we need to define rather more precisely what the fourth beast symbolises. We have seen that the fourth beast was killed *after* the little horn had been persecuting the saints for a period of time. If we regard the beast as symbolising the whole Greek empire, including Macedon and Egypt, we run into difficulty, because Rome conquered Macedon before Antiochus began persecuting the Jews in earnest. This diffi-culty immediately disappears when we recognise the obvious, namely, that the beast represents the *Syrian* part of the Greek empire. It includes the empire of Alexander, but following his death, Macedon and Egypt drop away out of sight, and Syria is pictured as the continuation of the empire. This is reason-able, because 1. the Syrian empire (and it *was* an empire) was the largest of the three, 2. it was the one which came to rule over the Jews and affected them most profoundly and 3. by virtue of its geographical location it was the successor of the Babylonian, Median and Persian empires. Bearing this in mind, we may now see how the three stages outlined earlier were fulfilled.

Stage 1. Judgment is passed upon the Syrian Greek empire and Antiochus. Faithful Jews, enabled by God and inspired by loyalty to their religion, rebel successfully against their Greek rulers and so deal a death blow to the Syrian Greek empire. At about the same time Antiochus is struck down by the hand of God, through a mysterious illness. (Note that these facts also explain the striking of the image on its feet of iron and clay by the stone. We shall see in the next chapter that 8:25 clearly indicates that Antiochus Epiphanes was struck down by the hand of God, and the wording of that verse links it closely to 2:34).

Stage 2. In time, Rome appears on the scene and annexes the Syrian empire. Thus is the 'body' of the beast destroyed (7:11). *Babylon, Media and Persia, however, all lie outside the borders of the Roman empire.* They are deprived of their authority, but they are independent of Rome. Thus is fulfilled the prediction, 'As for the rest of the beasts, their dominion was taken away, but their lives were prolonged for a season and a time' (7:12). We shall see later that these events are described in a very remarkable way in Daniel 11:40—45.

Stage 3. Christ performs His work on earth and then returns to Heaven to receive again dominion and glory, and the kingdom. The kingdom is also inherited by His 'body', the church, which is composed of His 'fellow heirs', the saints (Ephesians 1:18 — 2:6; Romans 8:16, 17).

'But you are a chosen race, a royal priesthood, a holy nation, God's own people . . .' (I Peter 2:9)

'. . . Jesus Christ the faithful witness, the first-born of the dead, and the ruler of kings on earth. To him who loves us and has freed us from our sins by his blood and made us a kingdom, priests to his God and Father . . .' (Revelation 1:5, 6)

'. . . thou wast slain, and didst purchase unto God with thy blood men of every tribe, and tongue, and people, and nation, and madest them to be unto our God a kingdom and priests; and they reign upon the earth.' (Revelation 5:9, 10, R.V.)[10]

We shall see later that these are not the only places in the book of Revelation where we are told that the saints are even now reigning with Christ (Revelation 20:4—6).

At this point let us turn briefly to Matthew 24:30, 31 where Christ appears to speak of the second advent and in doing so identifies Himself as the 'one like a son of man'.

'. . . then will appear the sign of the Son of man in heaven, and then all the tribes of the earth will mourn, and they will see the Son of man coming on the clouds of heaven with

---

10.   The Revised Version follows the best manuscripts in translating 'they reign upon the earth', rather than 'they shall reign on earth'.

power and great glory; and he will send out his angels with
a loud trumpet call, and they will gather his elect from the
four winds, from one end of heaven to the other.' (Matthew
24:30, 31)

As in the case of the stone, it may be contended that Christ
was speaking of the event in Daniel, which must therefore be
identified as a picture of the second advent. However, as in
the case of the stone, this is not necessarily so at all. Christ
was certainly *identifying* Himself as the 'one like a son of man'
by using language similar to that of Daniel, but He is not
necessarily speaking of the same event (assuming He is referring
to the second advent), as can be seen by simple comparison.
In Daniel's vision it is a *heavenly* (and therefore pictorially
represented) scene in which Christ is *brought before the
Ancient of Days and is given dominion and glory*. At the
second advent, however, Christ will be *literally and visibly*
appearing in the clouds of heaven, and He will be *coming to
meet His saints on earth*. He will *not,* at that time, be brought
before the Ancient of Days to be given dominion and glory,
because He is *already at the right hand of Power*. The latter
is shown by Matthew 26:64 and Luke 22:69.

'But I tell you, hereafter you will see the Son of man
seated at the right hand of Power, and coming on the clouds
of heaven.' (Matthew 26:64)

'But from now on the Son of man shall be seated at the
right hand of the power of God.' (Luke 22:69)

Both passages record Christ's words to the Sanhedrin shortly
before His crucifixion, and they are a clear allusion to Daniel
7:13, 14. The Greek *ap arti,* translated 'hereafter', means
'from now'. On this occasion, therefore, Christ did *not* identify
the scene in Daniel's vision as that of the second advent. He
clearly identified it as the scene of His triumphal return to
Heaven following the crucifixion and resurrection. At the
second advent, Jesus will come in the glory which He has
possessed since the time of the first advent.

We should add here a word of clarification about the symbolical nature of the language in these verses. When Jesus
said, 'Hereafter you will see the Son of man seated at the
right hand of Power, and coming on the clouds of heaven', He

did not of course mean that the Jews (of that time) would literally see Him thus with their physical eyes. Jesus is not seated on a literal, physical throne, and neither did He come to the Father on literal, physical clouds. The language employed is the 'technical language of prophecy', and is clearly symbolical. The clouds and the implied throne convey the idea of Christ's elevation to power and glory, but they are not meant to be taken literally, any more than the four beasts are. Jesus was simply saying that the Jews would see the *evidence* of His exaltation and power (particularly, perhaps, in the destruction of Jerusalem in 70 A.D.).

At this point we must return briefly to Matthew 24:30. We assumed above that this refers to the second advent. In fact, however, there are good reasons for believing that Jesus used Daniel 7:13, 14 *in its original sense* there, just as He did in Matthew 26:64. R. T. France argues convincingly that in Matthew 24:30 (or the parallel Mark 13:26) Jesus was not referring to the second advent — He was referring to the glorification and vindication which followed His resurrection.[11] The context indicates that Jesus could have been saying that He would be vindicated and His power revealed by the destruction of the Jewish nation in 70 A.D. In that case we should read, 'then all the tribes of the *land* will mourn'. The 'sign of the Son of man in heaven' — that is, the sign of Christ's exaltation and power — was His destruction of the nation in 70 A.D. Further on in this book we shall see how immensely important the events of 70 A.D. are in both the prophecies of Daniel and the teaching of Jesus.

This interpretation of Matthew 24:30 makes obvious sense of Christ's words in verse 34 — 'Truly, I say to you, this generation will not pass away till all these things take place.' Compare Matthew 16:28 — 'Truly, I say to you, there are some standing here who will not taste death before they see the Son of man coming in his kingdom.' Many may find this interpretation of Matthew 24:30 difficult to accept; but the meaning of Matthew 16:28 and 26:64 is perfectly plain.

11. *Jesus and the Old Testament*, by R. T. France, (Tyndale Press, 1971). See section on 'The Son of Man' (pp. 135—148) and on Mark 13:24—27 (pp. 227—239). See also the section on Matthew 24 in the Tyndale commentary on *Matthew*, by R. V. G. Tasker.

In those verses Jesus clearly applied Daniel 7:13, 14 to His own exaltation following His resurrection.

Remember, however, what we said in our introductory chapter about 'prophetic foreshortening'. Daniel's vision of the 'one like a son of man' refers primarily to Christ's first advent, but it looks beyond it to His second advent also. The vision does not distinguish between the two advents, because they are both parts of *one event* — namely, 'the coming of the Son of man'. This event covers the whole period of 'the time of the end' or 'the last days'. It began with the first advent, but it will be completed by the second advent.

The place of the Roman empire

Before going on, we shall pause briefly to consider Rome's place in the prophecies. We shall show that the Roman empire *has* a place in the prophecies' fulfilment — but it is a secondary fulfilment. It is not the primary fulfilment imagined by orthodox and dispensationalist interpreters.

A strong clue can be found in the book of Revelation, chapter 13, where John describes a great beast.

'And I saw a beast rising out of the sea with ten horns and seven heads, with ten diadems upon its horns and a blasphemous name upon its heads. And the beast that I saw was like a leopard, its feet were like a bear's, and its mouth was like a lion's mouth. And to it the dragon gave his power and his throne and great authority.' (Revelation 13:1, 2)

It is obvious that this beast is a combination of the four beasts described in Daniel 7. (Note that the four beasts had seven heads between them.) The beast partakes of many of the characteristics of Daniel's fourth beast, but it is a *composite* beast — it is not the same as the fourth beast.

Now the narrative indicates (as we shall see when we consider the matter more fully in our final chapter) that to some extent this beast symbolises *the Roman empire*. But it also symbolises other antichristian powers and organisations of the present age, including the last great 'Antichrist'. Thus the four great heathen pre-Christian empires of Babylon, Media, Persia and Greece *collectively symbolise and foreshadow* the anti-Christian powers and organisations of this present age — particularly the Roman empire.

Summary

At this point let us look back over Daniel's first two prophecies and summarise briefly. Both prophecies look forward to a heavenly, Messianic kingdom, and both indicate that this kingdom is to be preceded by four great earthly kingdoms. We have identified these four kingdoms as Babylon, Media, Persia and Greece, and we have done so for two main reasons: 1. The description of the four kingdoms is an exact description of Babylon, Media, Persia and Greece. 2. The New Testament indicates that the heavenly kingdom of both visions is that which was established by Christ some two thousand years ago. The vision of the image indicates that Christ *began* the process of setting up the kingdom by destroying the fourth empire — the feet of iron and clay were broken *before* the stone became a mountain. And the vision of the four beasts indicates that the fourth empire was completely destroyed *before* Christ was glorified after His crucifixion and resurrection. It follows that the fourth empire cannot be the Roman empire; it must be the Greek empire.

However, lest we should still be unable to make up our minds, the book of Daniel now proceeds to name these empires by name — as we shall see in the next chapter.

CHAPTER FOUR

The Ram and the He-Goat

In the eighth chapter of Daniel we find the record of a vision seen in about 550 B.C., the year in which Cyrus created the Persian empire. Daniel sees two beasts which are specifically identified as the Persian and Greek empires. His informant says,

> 'Understand, O son of man, that the vision is for the time of the end . . . Behold, I will make known to you what shall be at the latter end of the indignation; for it pertains to the appointed time of the end.' (Daniel 8:17, 19)

This third vision is similar to the earlier ones, and is clearly meant to help us with the identification of the four kingdoms. It concentrates almost entirely on a description of Greece and Antiochus Epiphanes — and the description corresponds closely to that of the fourth kingdom and little horn. The information that the vision concerns 'the time of the end' should be enough to clinch the matter. Unfortunately most conservative interpreters think otherwise. For this reason we shall have to go through the vision carefully and see just why it proves that the fourth kingdom is Greek. This is how it begins:

> 'In the third year of the reign of King Belshazzar a vision appeared to me, Daniel, after that which appeared to me at the first. And I saw in the vision; and when I saw, I was in Susa the capital, which is in the province of Elam; and I saw in the vision, and I was at the river Ulai. I raised my eyes and saw, and behold . . .'

The ram

> '. . . a ram standing on the bank of the river. It had two

horns; and both horns were high, but one was higher than the other, and the higher one came up last. I saw the ram charging westward and northward and southward; no beast could stand before him, and there was no one who could rescue from his power; he did as he pleased and magnified himself.' (Daniel 8:1—4)

Daniel's informant briefly explains,

'As for the ram which you saw with the two horns, these are the kings of Media and Persia.' (Daniel 8:20)

In this vision a clear distinction is made between Media and Persia. The kings of Media are said to arise first and become great. Afterwards the kings of Persia arise and become still greater. This acknowledges the fact that Media held the reins of power before Persia. However, the two horns are on one beast, signifying the fact that they became united as allies. Now it happens that the first two visions (i.e., those of the image and four beasts) were seen at a time when Media was a powerful, independent empire. The vision of the two-horned ram was seen at about the very time (550 B.C.) when Media and Persia became united under the role of Cyrus. It was therefore specially appropriate at that time to depict the Medes and Persians as united, the Persians being dominant.

Daniel begins his account of the vision by saying that he saw a two-horned ram in Elam (the land of Cyrus's origin). It is subsequently made clear that this ram represented the Persian-dominated Medo-Persian empire. *The two-horned ram therefore primarily refers to the empire created by Cyrus in 550 B.C.*

However, since one horn represents the kings of Media, the ram, superficially at least, appears to incorporate also the Median empire which preceded the Medo-Persian empire created by Cyrus. This point will be dealt with further in the next chapter, but let it be emphasised here that the beast *primarily pictures the empire created by Cyrus in 550 B.C.* The vision is seen in about 550 B.C. and the beast begins its activities from the land of Elam, after the rise of the Persian horn. All these details point to Cyrus's new empire. The exploits of the beast are entirely those of the Persian empire. The two horns indicate that in fact the kingdom consists of two different peoples, and that the inferior people itself possessed an empire before the rise of the superior race. We can say that the beast represents the Medo-Persian empire formed in 550 B.C., and that the description of the two horns is probably little more than a historical note about the two peoples brought together in that empire. The horns 1. tell us that the new empire is a partnership between the Medes and Persians, the latter being dominant, and 2. give us the interesting information that this Persian dominance was preceded by a Median dominance.

Having described the ram, Daniel goes on to show that it will launch out on an unchecked (and therefore probably rapid) campaign of conquest resulting in an empire of great size. No other kingdom will be able to withstand it. It will do what it likes and make itself great. Now it should be questioned which of the two middle kingdoms of the image and four beasts the ram resembles more closely — the second or the third kingdom?

The second kingdom was 'inferior' to Babylon. It was powerful and rapacious, but we have the impression that it was not a fast mover. A bear is bulky and relatively slow — particularly, perhaps, when it is a lop-sided bear! It was ordered to 'arise and devour much flesh', but we are not told whether it obeyed this command. The third kingdom moved swiftly, was given 'dominion' and 'ruled over all the earth'.

The reader will probably agree that the description of the third kingdom fits the ram better than that of the second. This would indicate that the third kingdom is the Persian empire. There is, however, at least one similarity between the ram and the bear (the second of the four kingdoms). The bear 'was raised up on one side', and of the ram's two horns, 'one was higher than the other'. There is undoubtedly a similarity here; but various considerations make it likely that although *there is a connection,* these two conditions of 'lop-sidedness' do not signify the same thing. A little further on in this chapter it will be shown that evidence for this can be found in Daniel 11.

The connection is the fact that in both cases the lopsidedness has something to do with the partnership between Media and Persia. The unequal height of the ram's horns speaks of

Persia's senior role in her partnership with Media. Recipro-
cally, the bear's one-sided elevation speaks of Media's early
supremacy, but later subordination when in partnership with
Persia. This suggestion is supported by 1. the fact that the
bear as a whole is best explained in terms of the Median
empire, and 2. the fact that the ram's exploits approximate
more closely to those of the third kingdom than those of the
second.

We conclude, therefore, that the Persian-dominated Medo-
Persian ram on the whole supports our identification of the
second kingdom as Media and the third as Persia. More will be
said about this part of the vision later.

The he-goat with a conspicuous horn

*'As I was considering, behold, a he-goat came from the
west across the face of the whole earth, without touching
the ground; and the goat had a conspicuous horn between
his eyes. He came to the ram with the two horns, which I
had seen standing on the bank of the river, and he ran at
him in his mighty wrath. I saw him come close to the ram,
and he was enraged against him and struck the ram and
broke his two horns; and the ram had no power to stand
before him, but he cast him down to the ground and
trampled upon him; and there was no one who could rescue
the ram from his power. Then the he-goat magnified himself
exceedingly; but when he was strong, the great horn was
broken, and instead of it there came up four conspicuous
horns toward the four winds of heaven.' (Daniel 8:5—8)*

Daniel's informant explains,

*'And the he-goat is the king of Greece; and the great horn
between his eyes is the first king. As for the horn that was
broken, in place of which four others arose, four kingdoms
shall arise from his nation, but not with his power.' (Daniel
8:21, 22)*

We have here a very vivid description of Greece's destruction
of the Persian empire. The fantastically swift progress and
irresistible power of the Greek armies is pictured in colourful
detail. The single great horn symbolises Alexander and the
four subsequent horns symbolise the four kingdoms founded

by the four generals who gained control of the Greek empire after the death of Alexander.

When we compare this picture of Greece with Daniel's four kingdoms, it is immediately obvious that there is a very striking similarity between this he-goat and the fourth kingdom. Let us list the similarities, quoting (a) details of the he-goat, followed by (b) details of the fourth kingdom.

1. a. 'came across the face of the whole earth'
   b. 'devour the whole earth'
2. a. 'his mighty wrath'
   b. 'terrible and dreadful and exceedingly strong'
3. a. 'struck the ram and broke his two horns'
   b. 'devoured and broke in pieces'
4. a. 'cast him down to the ground and trampled upon him'
   b. 'stamped the residue with its feet'

Greece and the fourth kingdom both had this initial phase of immense power, but they both had a second phase of division and weakness.

5. a. 'four kingdoms shall arise from his nation, but not with his power'
   b. 'it shall be a divided kingdom . . . partly strong and partly brittle'

It is quite obvious that the description of the fourth kingdom corresponds very closely indeed to that of the Greek he-goat. In the present writer's opinion, the two things are so manifestly parallel accounts that the fourth kingdom must be identified as the Greek empire. It is not denied that there are also certain similarities between the he-coat and the third kingdom, but they are all features which Greece and Persia just happened to have in common — that is, 'four kings' (or kingdoms) and a large empire. Swiftness of movement is also suggested by the appearance of the third beast, though this is not specifically mentioned. Regarding the four heads and horns, it should be noted that the four heads of the leopard were prominent features of its *dominion,* whereas the four horns of the Greek he-goat are associated with a very marked *decrease* in dominion. The leopard's heads appear to be connected with an initial phase of power and expansion, whereas the he-goat's horns are connected with a secondary phase of

division and weakness. This indicates that the four heads of
the leopard are to be identified *not* with the four horns of the
he-goat, but rather with the four kings of Persia mentioned in
Daniel 10:1 and 11:2.

In these two verses we are told about the *four* powerful
kings who created the Persian empire. Almost immediately
afterwards, in 11:4, we are told about Alexander's Greek
empire being broken and divided, after his death, toward the
four winds of heaven. The natural conclusion is that the
leopard's four heads represent the kings of Persia, whereas the
he-goat's four horns represent something entirely different —
namely, the four kingdoms into which the Greek empire was
divided after Alexander's death. This has a bearing on the
interpretation of one of the other beasts also. Namely, the
bear. We have seen that the he-goat's four horns have nothing
whatever to do with the leopard's four heads. In a similar
way — if our interpretation is correct — the unequal horns of
the ram do *not* signify the same thing as the unequal sides of
the bear. There is a connection, however, since in both cases
the inequality has something to do with the partnership between the Medes and Persians.

The little horn

'Out of one of them (the four horns) came forth a little
horn, which grew exceedingly great toward the south, toward the east, and toward the glorious land. It grew great,
even to the host of heaven; and some of the host of the
stars it cast down to the ground, and trampled upon them.
It magnified itself, even up to the Prince of the host; and
the continual burnt offering was taken away from him, and
the place of his sanctuary was overthrown. And the host
was given over to it together with the continual burnt
offering through transgression; and truth was cast down to
the ground, and the horn acted and prospered. Then I heard
a holy one speaking; and another holy one said to the one
that spoke, "For how long is the vision concerning the continual burnt offering, the transgression that makes desolate,
and the giving over of the sanctuary and host to be
trampled under foot?". And he said to him, "For two
thousand and three hundred evenings and mornings; then*

the sanctuary shall be restored to its rightful state".'
(Daniel 8:9—14)

Daniel's informant, the angel Gabriel, explains,

*'And at the latter end of their (the four kingdoms') rule,
when the transgressors have reached their full measure, a
king of bold countenance, one who understands riddles,
shall arise. His power shall be great, and he shall cause
fearful destruction, and shall succeed in what he does, and
destroy mighty men and the people of the saints. By his
cunning he shall make deceit prosper under his hand, and
in his own mind he shall magnify himself. Without warning
he shall destroy many; and he shall even rise up against the
Prince of princes; but, by no human hand, he shall be
broken.' (Daniel 8:23—25)*

In these passages we have a description of Antiochus
Epiphanes. There can be no doubt about this whatsoever. The
following brief outline should make this clear.

After Alexander died, his empire broke up and his generals
fought over the remains. Following the battle of Ipsus, four
generals emerged as the most powerful rulers. Cassander held
sway in Greece and Macedonia, Lysimachus in Thrace and part
of Asia Minor, Ptolemy in Egypt, Palestine etc. and Seleucus
in Syria, Babylonia, Media etc.

Over the years of Greek rule, there was a falling away from
God in Israel. Many succumbed to the Greek culture and were
also willing to compromise in the matter of religion. This was
open transgression of God's law and was a sin which steadily
increased, involving more and more people. And so it was
that 'when the transgressors had reached their full measure'
Antiochus Epiphanes became king of Syria. He was a member
of the Seleucid dynasty and by means of great cunning and
craftiness he raised himself from a position of no importance
to one of great power. His campaigns carried him eastwards
into Babylonia etc. and southwards into Egypt and Judaea,
'the glorious land'.

He made it part of his policy to stamp out the Jewish
religion. He deliberately set himself against all faithful Jews
('the host of heaven', 'the people of the saints'), savagely
persecuting both the people and their leaders ('the stars'). The

first to fall was the high priest himself, Onias, in 170 B.C. In pursuing this policy Antiochus set himself against the God of Heaven who was in theory the ruler of this theocratic state and in fact the ruler of those Jews who were godly ('the Prince of the host' and 'Prince of princes'). From what will be said in this and a later chapter, it will become apparent that this 'Prince' is Christ Himself. As described already, Antiochus magnified himself to such an extent that he called himself God. He desecrated the temple, caused the daily sacrifices to cease and finally placed in the temple an altar for the worship of Olympian Zeus, whose incarnation he claimed to be.

However, the persecutions of Antiochus stimulated a heroic resistance. Faithful Jews preferred to endure the most bestial tortures and a lingering death rather than betray their faith. The more warlike rallied to the banner of Judas Maccabeus and defeated the armies of Antiochus again and again. In December, 164 B.C. the temple was recovered, cleansed and rededicated, and the 'continual burnt offering' was restored. The time between the death in 170 B.C. of Onias, the first of the host to be cast down, and the cleansing of the temple was probably just about 2300 days, a period of between six and seven years.

Antiochus's fury knew no bounds when he heard of the Jews' successes. He was on campaign in the East at the time, but he hastened back, vowing to slaughter the Jews mercilessly. But the 'Prince of princes' struck first. Antiochus died an unpleasant death, apparently by worms and ulcers. In this the Jews saw the hand of God.

The overall effect of Antiochus's persecution and the faithful Jews' resistance was to weed out the 'transgressors' or Hellenising Jews, and to purify religion. The latter Jews had sympathised with Antiochus's aims and actually assisted him in his sacriligious activities. The transgressors had indeed 'reached their full measure'.

Now it is clear that there is a close similarity between this description of Antiochus and that of the little horn in chapter 7. The similarity is so obvious that many people believe Antiochus to be a type of 'The Antichrist' (which is what they take the little horn of chapter 7 to represent). And indeed

Antiochus may be such; but *not* because the little horn of chapter 7 directly refers to the Antichrist. Both little horns specifically refer to *Antiochus,* although he himself may well be a type of some future antichrist (see II Thessalonians 2:1— 12). Let us list the similarities between the two 'little horns' —

1. Both horns arise out of a great empire during a second phase of division and weakness, the first phase being one of immense power and destructiveness.
2. Both horns become great from small beginnings.
3. Both horns persecute and prevail over the saints.
4. The first horn speaks 'great things and words against the Most High' and the second horn 'magnified itself, even up to the Prince of the host'.
5. Both horns have power over certain ordinances. The specific mention of the removal of the daily sacrifice in this chapter tends to confirm the interpretation we put on Daniel 7:25 ('He shall . . . think to change the times and the law; and they shall be given into his hand for a time, two times, and a division of a time'). The longer period of time mentioned in this chapter (2300 days) covers the period during which both the sanctuary *and the host* are trodden under foot.[1] Antiochus himself was not directly responsible for the death of Onias, and it occurred before the full storm of persecution fell upon the saints. Nevertheless his death was a direct result of Antiochus's policy of meddling in Jewish religious affairs and was the first, and by no means insignificant, ripple preceding the tidal wave that followed.
6. Both horns oppose God and are destroyed *by God. We have in this chapter a very dramatic confirmation of the statement made earlier on, that the fourth kingdom (and therefore also the little horn) is destroyed by the pre-*

1. Some interpreters try to bring this figure closer to the 'three and a division times' of chapter 7 and 1290 days of chapter 12 by asserting that it means 2300 half days or 1150 full days. This is unnecessary, unsatisfactory and probably incorrect. The expression 'evening-morning' (as it translates literally) is probably based on Genesis 1, and therefore means one day.

incarnate Christ. We are told here that Antiochus rises
up against the 'Prince of princes', but is broken 'by no
human hand' (literally 'without hand', as in the R.V.).
This Prince of princes can be none other, surely, than
Jesus Christ Himself — the King of kings and Lord of lords
(Revelation 17:14; 19:16). *His* was the divine hand
that struck Antiochus down. This is entirely compatible
with the teaching of the New Testament. We read in
Colossians 1:16, 17, 'For in him all things were created
. . . whether thrones or dominions'. Not only does Christ
create thrones and dominions, but He also destroys them.
Compare the statement that Antiochus opposes the
Prince of princes, but is broken 'by no human hand' with
the statement that the fourth kingdom is broken by a
stone cut out 'by no human hand' (2:34). Further proof
that this Prince is Christ will be given in a later chapter.

In conclusion, it is clear that the ram and he-goat resemble
the third and fourth kingdoms far more than the second and
third kingdoms. No person can reasonably deny this. Orthodox
and dispensationalist interpreters pick out the differences
between the two little horns and inform us that these prove
beyond doubt that the two horns do not symbolise the same
person. They point out, for instance, that the first little horn
comes up after ten other horns, uprooting three in the process,
whereas the second little horn grows out of one of four horns.
Such reasoning is really most odd! Of course there are differences — there is no point in having a second vision if it
reveals exactly the same details as the first vision. In the
second vision a different symbol is used to bring out further
details. The different details in the two visions are all equally
true of Antiochus. In the first vision it is revealed that he
will be preceded by a line of seven kings (the Seleucids of
Syria), which will arise from the empire of Alexander, and
that he will uproot a further three during his rise to power.
In the second vision it is further revealed that the kingdom
out of which he arises (Seleucid Syria) will in fact be one of a
group of four kingdoms which arise out of Alexander's empire
(Macedonia, Thrace, Syria and Egypt).

Thus some of the details about the little horn in chapter 7
are reiterated in chapter 8 and further details are added. An

even fuller description of the Greek empire and Antiochus is given in chapter 11. The progression of the revelation is unmistakable. In each succeeding vision we are given a fuller description of an empire which will precede the arrival of the Messiah. In order that no mistake may be made, a particular king is described in great detail. The vision culminates in the revelation of chapter 11, where we find a fantastically detailed account of Greek history from Alexander the Great to the destruction of the Greek empire by Rome. It includes an account of Antiochus Epiphanes which takes up nineteen verses.

In the first two visions the fourth empire is described in very considerable detail. Our attention is *specially focussed* on that empire and the little horn, and Daniel himself takes an intense interest in them (7:19, 20). The reason for this is, presumably, the fact that the fourth empire immediately precedes the kingdom of Heaven. The following visions of chapters 8 and 11 are almost entirely devoted to a detailed and lengthy description of the *Greek* empire and Antiochus Epiphanes. The way in which this description corresponds to the fourth empire is so overwhelmingly obvious, it is surprising that many interpreters seriously prefer to believe that in fact it describes the third empire. That the immensely important fourth empire is being identified before our very eyes is by far and away the most likely explanation. It is being named by name.

Finally, let us again note these words concerning the vision of the ram and the he-goat:

> '*Understand, O son of man, that the vision is for the time of the end... Behold, I will make known to you what shall be at the latter end of the indignation; for it pertains to the appointed time of the end . . . but seal up the vision, for it pertains to many days hence.*' *(Daniel 8:17, 19, 26)*

This categorically states that the 'time of the end' will be associated with the Greek empire and the destruction of Antiochus. Orthodox and other interpreters get round this by saying that Greece and Antiochus 'pertain to the time of the end' only in the sense that they are 'types' of the fourth empire and the little horn. They themselves are to be identified with the third empire, but they are types of the fourth. What an extraordinary interpretation! How unnecessarily complicated! The simple meaning of the words is that Greece itself, preceded by the Persian empire, 'pertains to the time of the end'.

The visions we have now considered give a very clear picture of world history from the time of Daniel to the coming of the Messiah. The kingdom which preceded the heavenly kingdom has not only been described in considerable detail; it has been named by name. At this point the book of Daniel switches over and pinpoints the coming of the Messiah from a different angle. This time the reader is enabled to calculate the *actual date* of the Messiah's appearance.

But before we go on to study chapter 9, we must take a closer look at the Medo-Persian problem. It is generally stated that there was no genuine Median empire between the Babylonian and Persian empires, and conservative interpreters also claim that Media and Persia cannot be separated. Largely because of this, so the present writer believes, a series of comparatively straightforward prophecies has been converted into a dust-filled battle field. The question of Media's place in the prophecies lies at the root of most of the trouble.

CHAPTER FIVE

The Medes and Persians

The Medo-Persian problem is a subject which needs a chapter to itself. The problem is **a.** the question of whether Daniel separates the Medes and Persians or whether he only considers them as one nation, and **b.** the question of whether there was a genuine Median kingdom between those of Babylon and Persia. The latter question has been dealt with already; so in this chapter we shall concentrate mainly on the former.

What the Bible says

Before we consider what Daniel says, let us see what earlier prophets say concerning the downfall of Babylon.

'The Lord has stirred up the spirit of the kings of the Medes, because his purpose concerning Babylon is to destroy it . . .' (Jeremiah 51:11)

'Prepare the nations for war against her, the kings of the Medes, with their governors and deputies, and every land under their dominion.' (Jeremiah 51:28)

'Behold, I am stirring up the Medes against them . . .' (Isaiah 13:17)

'Go up, O Elam, lay siege, O Media . . .' (Isaiah 21:2)

These passages single out Media as the nation which God would stir up against Babylon, but as noted in an earlier chapter, we are told that Elam also would be involved in its actual overthrow. Eastern Elam was occupied by the Persian race at this time and was Cyrus's place of origin. He succeeded his father on the throne of Anshan, but soon added the province of Persia to his possessions. He overthrew the Median king and in partnership with the Medes eventually conquered Babylon.

Now Daniel appears to support these prophecies, because he makes a special point of repeatedly emphasising that Darius, the new king of Babylon, is a Mede.

'And Darius the Mede received the kingdom . . .' (Daniel 5:+!)

'. . . Darius the son of Ahasuerus, by birth a Mede, who became king over the realm of the Chaldeans . . .' (Daniel 9:1)

'. . . Darius the Mede . . .' (Daniel 11:1)

Daniel states clearly that Babylon is conquered by the allied Medes and Persians (5:28; 6:8), but he emphasises that the new king is a *Mede*. We are given the *impression* (whatever the precise situation may have been) that the Babylonian kings were succeeded by a Median king and then the Persian kings. This is only a superficial impression (as will be shown further on in this chapter), but it may well be intentional. The book of Daniel seems to be making a curious and unmistakable point of emphasising and spotlighting the part played by Media in the early administration of Babylon, following the latter's defeat. This suggests that the book intends Media to be regarded as the successor of Babylon. We are not saying that the kingdom of Darius *was* the Median kingdom. We are merely suggesting that the book of Daniel uses Darius to get across the idea that Media was the second of the four world powers.

The vision of the ram and the he-goat shows that in fact Persia was dominant when Babylon was finally overthrown; but as noted already, the second kingdom did not begin with Babylon's final overthrow. *It began with the end of Nebuchadnezzar's reign.* The first kingdom's period of power corresponds only to the empire of Nebuchadnezzar. In the vision of the image, the first kingdom is specifically identified with Nebuchadnezzar himself. The second vision points to the same person without actually naming him. Interpreters usually, if not always, assume that Nebuchadnezzar represents the whole Neo-Babylonian empire. This assumption would be quite reasonable if it were not for the existence of the Medo-Persian problem. The question of whether or not the first kingdom's power is limited to the time of Nebuchadnezzar is crucial – and the Bible is absolutely specific in stating that the first kingdom is to be identified with Nebuchadnezzar himself. This totally invalidates the objection that there was no Median empire between those of Babylon and Persia.

It is said by some interpreters that because Daniel never specifically mentions an independent Median empire, the second of his kingdoms cannot have been that empire. Note, however, that Daniel had little or no personal contact with Media during her short period of supreme power, and also 2:39 indicates that the second kingdom was relatively insignificant. It is not surprising, therefore, that Daniel makes little mention of independent Media. We say 'little' mention, because he does refer to the independent Median empire in the vision of the ram and the he-goat. He tells us that he saw a ram with two horns. He sees that both horns are high, but one is higher than the other, and the higher came up last. The explanation that Daniel is given contains a direct reference to the Median empire which preceded the Persian empire. He is told that one horn represents the kings of Media. This horn came up *first* and must therefore represent the kings of *the Median empire*. The other horn represents the kings of Persia. The latter horn came up after the first horn and must therefore represent the kings of the Persian empire.

However, orthodox interpreters rightly point out that these Median and Persian horns both appear on one beast. This has already been discussed in the previous chapter; but more can be said. It is clear that the ram is primarily meant to symbolise the Medo-Persian empire created by Cyrus in 550 B.C. – it was initially described as a two-horned ram standing in Elam, the land of Cyrus's origin, in about 550 B.C. But it does also refer to the earlier supremacy of Media. Orthodox interpreters conclude therefore that the Medes and Persians are here considered to be one people, both before and after 550 B.C. – that is, during the years of both the Median empire and the Medo-Persian empire. This conclusion could be correct as far as it goes; but these interpreters go further. They insist that because *this* vision appears to depict the Medes and Persians as one people throughout their history, they must likewise be considered one people in the other visions also. They insist that Media and Persia can never be separated — Media must always be considered a part of Medo-Persia.

In a certain very limited sense, perhaps, the Medes and Persians *were* always a unity. They were of similar racial stock, lived similar steppe-dwelling lives and were geographical neighbours. In this sense we could perhaps say they were a unity even before the time of Cyrus. This truth (as well as the partnership created by Cyrus) *may* be symbolised by the two-horned ram. It is also true, however, that the Medes and Persians were two quite distinct and separate peoples with different empires. There is no good reason why this latter truth should not have been symbolised in the visions of the image and four beasts, and the former truth in the vision of the ram. The bear and leopard could have symbolised one truth and the two-horned ram another truth.

Daniel saw the vision of the ram in the third year of the reign of Belshazzar (about 550 B.C.), *the very time at which the Medes and Persians united as allies.* Cyrus's amalgamation of Media and Persia was a very excellent reason for altering the symbolism in such a way as to depict the unity of the Medes and Persians. When the visions of the image and four beasts were seen, Media was a powerful independent empire; but when Daniel saw the vision of the ram and he-goat, *the Medo-Persian situation had completely changed* (or was just about to), and a change of symbolism was altogether appropriate.

It has already been shown in the previous chapter that the description of the two horns is, in any case, probably little more than an historical note about the two peoples brought together in Cyrus's empire. Those who seek to prove the orthodox interpretation by emphasising the unity of the Medes and Persians in the ram tend to overlook the fact that the beast *primarily represents the empire created by Cyrus.* It is doubtful whether the ram is meant to show, even in a minor sense, that the Medes and Persians were always united. But whichever way we take it, the vision is quite compatible with the Babylon-Media-Persia-Greece interpretation.

To summarise, we can say that through Darius the Mede Daniel consistently depicts the Medes as following the Babylonians. In this he is supported by the prophets Isaiah and Jeremiah. In the vision of the ram he directly refers to the Median empire which preceded the Medo-Persian empire. It is true that he depicts the Medes and Persians as one people in this vision; but this is simply because they were at that very time uniting under the leadership of Cyrus. The vision clearly indicates that Persian rule was preceded by Median rule.

Further implications of Daniel 8

We have argued that the vision of the ram and the he-goat differs from the earlier visions in depicting a united Medo-Persia. We have also noted that this vision was seen at about the very time when the two nations actually united.

This change of symbolism at this particular time is in fact a remarkable touch of authenticity which supports the book's claim that it was written in the sixth century B.C. If the author lived in the second century B.C. and was as confused about Medo-Persian history as the critics say he was, how did he manage to give the vision this particular date? And how did he know that it was the third year of the reign of Belshazzar? Belshazzar was someone the Greek historians had never even heard of.

This vision does not support the critical view that Daniel was confused about Medo-Persian history. According to the critics, the author inserted the Median kingdom (which they identify with the kingdom of Darius) between the reigns of Belshazzar and Cyrus. But as we have seen, the book of Daniel clearly indicates that Babylon was overthrown by a united Medo-Persia (5:28; 6:8). Furthermore, the vision of chapter 8 clearly indicates that the *Persians* were dominant in this partnership. And more than this, it indicates the actual year in which they became dominant! Is it just a coincidence that the vision took place in the third year of Belshazzar — the very time when Cyrus conquered the Medes and established his empire?

In fact his vision provides an important clue which helps us to solve the problem of Media's place in the prophecies. As we have seen, chapter 8 indicates that Daniel had a vision in which the first thing he saw (apart from certain geographical details) was a newly-formed Persian empire on the threshold of conquest. The vision took place in about 550 B.C., the very year in which the Persian empire actually was created. The vision was therefore a prophecy of what was going to happen *from that very time.* If the dominance of Persia was just beginning, then *the dominance of Babylon and Media must have passed already.* The first kingdom (Babylon) had already been identified with Nebuchadnezzar, therefore the dominance of Media must have extended from the death of Nebuchadnezzar in 562 B.C. to the rise of Persia in 550 B.C.

Why include the Median empire?

In spite of all this, one is still left with the feeling that it would have been simpler to have only three kingdoms, instead of four — that is, Babylon, Medo-Persia and Greece. Why do the visions of the image and the four beasts complicate the issue by bringing in the Median empire at all? It could have been left out quite easily without damaging the picture of the historical setting of Christ's coming. This question has been dealt with already in chapter 2. *The pattern of four successive ages, symbolised by metals of diminishing strength or value, was already in existence* — in the work of the eighth century Greek poet Hesiod, for example. God chose to take symbolism which was already well known in the ancient world, and to adapt and use it for His own purposes. By using the imagery of secular literature, God was showing that human, secular history is controlled by Him and is leading up to the consummation ordained by Him. God is in control, and His triumph and the eventual vindication of His saints is certain.

However, this still leaves us with the question, 'Why did God choose Greece to be the fourth kingdom, and not Rome?'. If Rome were the fourth we would have our four kingdoms without having to separate Media and Persia. The answer probably lies in the facts 1. that the Greek king Antiochus Epiphanes made a deliberate attempt to stamp out true religion, and it was natural to see the hand of God in his defeat and death, and 2. that the destruction of the Greek empire was followed by the coming of Christ and His kingdom. Apart from predicting the historical setting of Christ's coming, the prophecies were meant to show that the kingdoms of this world would be destroyed by God and followed by His everlasting kingdom. Bound up with this is the probability that these events of a past age are meant to typify events immediately preceding Christ's second advent. The book of Revelation seems to indicate that the second advent also will be preceded by a period of greatly increased persecution of God's people — possibly by some Antiochus-like 'Antichrist'.

The Roman empire completely fails to meet these criteria. When Christ came, the Roman empire was still expanding and full of vigour. It reached its greatest extent and was at the zenith of its power more than a century *after* the birth of Christ. Even then, it was another three hundred years before the western empire collapsed. The eastern part of the empire went on for another thousand years. Furthermore, both parts of the empire were nominally Christian when they fell.

Critical scholars have their own explanation as to why Greece was chosen as the fourth empire; but enough has been said about this in our introductory chapter. We can say in conclusion that the separation of Media and Persia in chapters 2 and 7 is fully compatible with their union in chapters 5, 6 and 8, and involves no inconsistency or self-contradiction.

What non-Biblical records say

Having seen what the Bible says, let us see what other historical records tell us.

The Medes and Chaldeans together broke the power of Assyria when they destroyed Nineveh in 612 B.C. Assyria was finally obliterated when Harran fell to the Chaldeans in 610 B.C. and the Assyrians failed to recapture it in 609 B.C. The Chaldeans took the Land of the Two Rivers and Syria-Palestine, forming the Neo-Babylonian empire, whilst the Medes established a powerful empire to the North and East.

The Median empire was a constant threat to the wealthier Babylonian empire, but while Nebuchadnezzar was king, Babylon was rich and strong. After Nebuchadnezzar's death in 562 B.C. Babylon declined, and *Media became the dominant power.* Nabonidus, the last king of Babylon, tried to stave off the threat from Media by forming an alliance with the small, but growing, kingdom of Persia (a vassal of Media), whose ruler was Cyrus. However, a certain section of the Medians revolted against Astyages, the king of Media, in favour of Cyrus, who was related to the royal house of Media either by descent or marriage. Thus Cyrus, in alliance with these Medians, defeated Astyages in 550 B.C. and was installed as 'king of the Medes' (a title ascribed to him by Nabonidus). Cyrus adopted the Median royal regalia and settled for a time in Ecbatana, the Median capital. He placed both Medes and Persians in positions of high authority. Thus Media and Persia were united as allies. From this time, however, the Persians increased in power until they became completely dominant. We can see therefore that there was a Median empire and a Persian empire, but during the earlier years of the latter empire, the Medes were the allies of the Persians rather than their subjects.

Cyrus continued his triumphant progress and defeated Lydia in 546 B.C. and, after other conquests in the East, Babylon in 539 B.C. Immediately after defeating Babylon he appointed a man named Gubaru (not to be confused with the Ugbaru who captured Babylon) as governor of 'Babylon and the land beyond the river'. Gubaru in turn appointed sub-governors. This man Gubaru may have been either a Mede or a Persian, as Cyrus had a habit of appointing both Medes and Persians to positions of high authority. It is clear from various tablets the archaeologists have unearthed that Gubaru exercised very considerable authority within his vast satrapy of 'Babylon and the land beyond the river'. In fact it may truly be said that within his satrapy he exercised the authority of a king, although he remained subordinate to the higher authority of Cyrus and, later, Cambyses. In 530 B.C. Cyrus died on campaign in the far North East and his son Cambyses became head of the Persian empire. He proceeded to add Egypt to the territory of the empire, but in 522 B.C., on the way back from the campaign, he committed suicide when he heard that a pretender had taken the throne in his absence. This man claimed to be a brother of Cambyses who had actually been killed some time previously. However, within two months a cousin of Cambyses named Darius succeeded in capturing and killing the pretender. During his reign, Darius was succeeded in 486 B.C. by his son Xerxes. This man was notable for his invasion of Greece. He moved into that country with a huge army, but after some initial successes he was crushingly defeated in successive battles and forced out of Europe. He was eventually assassinated in 465 B.C. and succeeded by a son, Artaxerxes Longimanus.

The most striking aspect of the Persian empire was the fantastically large area it covered. The previous empires had all been but a fraction of the size of this vast structure. It reached its greatest extent during the reigns of Darius and Xerxes and its decline can be dated from the latter's defeat by the Greeks. Its period of greatness therefore covered the reigns of its first four kings, Cyrus, Cambyses, Darius and Xerxes.

Summary

It is clear that the picture Daniel gives is completely accurate in every detail except, apparently, that of Darius the Mede. Neither the Greek historians nor the cuneiform tablets make any mention of a king by this name who ruled in Babylon from 539 B.C. Consequently critical scholars regard Darius the Mede as a figment of the author's fertile imagination — or a 'conflation of confused traditions', to quote H. H. Rowley.[1] However, J. C. Whitcomb has paid careful attention to the findings of archaeology and has shown that there is good reason to believe that Darius the Mede was actually Gubaru, the governor of Babylon.[2]

Daniel calls Darius a 'king', but perhaps merely in the sense that he also calls Belshazzar the 'king'. Belshazzar exercised the *authority* of a king in Babylon, although he remained subordinate to his father Nabonidus, and is always called 'the son of the king' in the cuneiform records — never 'the king'. That Belshazzar was the second ruler in Babylonia is, however, revealed by the fact that he was not able to offer Daniel a position higher than that of the third ruler in the kingdom (5:7, 16, 29). Similarly, the fact that Darius 'received' the kingdom (5:31) and 'was made' king (9:1, R.V.) may indicate that he also occupied a subordinate position. As far as their subjects were concerned, however, Belshazzar and Gubaru wielded the authority of the kings who had reigned before

1. *Darius the Mede and the Four World Empires in the Book of Daniel*, by H. H. Rowley (Cardiff, 1935).

2. *Darius the Mede*, by J. C. Whitcomb (Eerdmans, 1959).

them. Thus when Daniel describes Darius as the king, it is quite possible that he is merely according him the title he was popularly known by in the realm of Babylon and the land beyond the river. He does not tell us what his official Persian title was, as he uses the Aramaic word for 'king', but he does give us the official Persian title of the sub-governors (satraps) he appointed.

We may well ask why Daniel chooses not to mention the fact that Darius was (if he was Gubaru) himself a governor appointed by the Persian Cyrus. It cannot be denied that the effect is one of making Media appear to be the successor of Babylon. The facts are all perfectly accurate, but they seem to be presented in such a way as to convey the idea of a Babylon-Media-Persia sequence.

The main problem with the Gubaru theory is the matter of the name. Why is the man called Darius rather than Gubaru? One suggestion is that he did in fact have both names. Another suggestion is that 'Darius' is here a scribal corruption of 'Gubaru'.[3] It should be mentioned that among other theories there is one that Darius the Mede may have been Cyrus himself.[4] In the present writer's opinion this is unlikely, but if it were true it would make Daniel's insistence on his Median origin even more strange and doubly significant. Despite his Median connections, Cyrus was undoubtedly a Persian, and is always depicted as such by the Bible. Whatever the correct answer may be, we can trust that time will yet again prove 'the Bible was right after all'. This is what happened with regard to Belshazzar, whose existence used to be denied by the critics — until the archaeologists found out who he was. Far from indicating the unreliability of the book of Daniel, Belshazzar now helps to show that it is both reliable and of ancient origin. The writer clearly had a much closer acquaintance with Babylonian times than did the Greek historians. The latter were unaware that Belshazzar even existed.

According to the Greek historians, Babylon was captured

3. This theory is set out in an unpublished manuscript by H. Owen, now deposited at the Tyndale House Library, Cambridge.

4. See article by D. J. Wiseman in *Notes on some Problems in the Book of Daniel*, Tyndale Press.

by a Babylonian named Gobryas, who had defected to Cyrus. This man was then appointed governor of 'Babylon and the land beyond the river'. The cuneiform records have revealed, however, that the Greek historians were wrong. Babylon was captured by a man named Ugbaru (who may have been the above-mentioned Babylonian); but he died three weeks later, and it was a different person, Gubaru, who became the governor. It is extremely likely that this Gubaru was none other than 'Darius the Mede'.

It is quite extraordinary how the critics have failed to learn from the affair of Belshazzar, and have continued to insist that Darius the Mede cannot have been a historical person. The confirmation of Belshazzar's existence teaches us at least two things relevant to the problem of Darius the Mede. One is that the author of the book of Daniel had very special knowledge of people and events around the time of the fall of Babylon — knowledge which the Greek historians did not possess. The other is that we should be very cautious about saying that a Biblical statement is inaccurate, or that a Biblical character is unhistorical. Archaeology is constantly bringing new evidence to light — and quite frequently it confirms the truth of Biblical statements which were previously uncorroborated or thought to be inaccurate.

Darius the Mede has not yet been identified with absolute certainty; but there is every reason to believe that he was a historical person, and that the author of the book of Daniel knew exactly what he was writing about when he described the Medes and Persians.

CHAPTER SIX

The Seventy Weeks

We now come to the ninth chapter of Daniel — the chapter which contains perhaps the most wonderful and dramatic prophecy of the book. The present writer believes that we are told the actual year of the Messiah's arrival, together with many details about His work of salvation. We are also given details about the destruction of Jerusalem in 70 A.D.

The chapter begins with the following words:

'In the first year of Darius the son of Ahasuerus, by birth a Mede, who became king over the realm of the Chaldeans — in the first year of his reign, I, Daniel, perceived in the books the number of years which, according to the word of the Lord to Jeremiah the prophet, must pass before the end of the desolations of Jerusalem, namely, seventy years. Then I turned my face to the Lord God, seeking him by prayer and supplications with fasting and sackcloth and ashes.' (Daniel 9:1—3)

Daniel's prayer

At this point Daniel begins to pray. He confesses the sins of his people and he confesses that they deserve their sufferings — the very sufferings of which God has warned them through Moses. He then prays,

'And now, O Lord our God, who didst bring thy people out of the land of Egypt with a mighty hand, and hast made thee a name, as at this day, we have sinned, we have done wickedly. O Lord, according to all thy righteous acts, let thy anger and thy wrath turn away from thy city Jerusalem, thy holy hill; because for our sins, and for the iniquities of our fathers, Jerusalem and thy people have

become a byword among all who are round about us. Now therefore, O our God, hearken to the prayer of thy servant and to his supplications, and for thy own sake, O Lord, cause thy face to shine upon thy sanctuary, which is desolate. O my God, incline thy ear and hear; open thy eyes and behold our desolations, and the city which is called by thy name; for we do not present our supplications before thee on the ground of our righteousness, but on the ground of thy great mercy. O Lord, hear; O Lord, forgive; O Lord, give heed and act; delay not, for thy own sake, O my God, because thy city and thy people are called by thy name.' (Daniel 9:15—19)

We must now look at the prophecy of which Daniel is speaking, and understand why it provokes this impassioned prayer.

'Therefore thus says the Lord of hosts: Because you have not obeyed my words, behold, I will send for all the tribes of the north, says the Lord, and for Nebuchadnezzar the king of Babylon, my servant, and I will bring them against this land and its inhabitants, and against all these nations round about; I will utterly destroy them, and make them a horror, a hissing, and an everlasting reproach . . . This whole land shall become a ruin and a waste, and these nations shall serve the king of Babylon seventy years. Then after seventy years are completed, I will punish the king of Babylon and that nation, the land of the Chaldeans, for their iniquity, says the Lord, making the land an everlasting waste. (Jeremiah 25:8—12)

'For thus says the Lord: When seventy years are completed for Babylon, I will visit you, and I will fulfil to you my promise and bring you back to this place.' (Jeremiah 29:10)

Let us make a list of the points we find in these prophecies:

1. Nebuchadnezzar and his people shall come against Judah and the surrounding nations and destroy them and make them a desolation.

2. These nations shall serve the king of Babylon for seventy years.

3. At the end of seventy years the king of Babylon and his

people shall be punished. Their land shall become desolate for ever.

4. After the completion of Babylon's seventy years of supremacy, God shall cause the Jews to return to their own land.

Let us now see how these prophecies were fulfilled:

1. In the same year that the prophecy was uttered (605 B.C.), Nebuchadnezzar came against Jerusalem, besieged it and took a number of hostages, including Daniel himself (Daniel 1:1, 2; II Kings 24:1). Jerusalem was again besieged in 597 B.C. and more Jews were exiled (II Kings 24:8—17). Finally Jerusalem was completely destroyed in 587 or 586 B.C. and more Jews were exiled (II Kings 25:1—22). The surrounding nations received similar treatment.

2, 3. Although Judah came under the Babylonian heel in 605 B.C., Babylon's ruling of nations actually dated from the overthrow of Assyria a few years earlier. After the fall of Ninevah in 612 B.C. (to the allied Medes and Babylonians), Ashur-uballit established his government at Harran. This city fell to the Babylonians in 610 B.C., and Assyria was finally obliterated when Ashur-uballit failed to recapture it in 609 B.C. *Seventy years* after she had finally conquered and destroyed Assyria, Babylon herself was conquered by Cyrus in 539 B.C. Since then Babylon has fallen into decay, and for many centuries it has been a desolate waste.

In Jeremiah 29:10 we are told that seventy years would be 'completed for Babylon'. This suggests that the full period of seventy years is to be identified with *Babylon's period of power*. The nations bordering Judah did not serve Babylon for quite the *full* period of seventy years, but there were other peoples who did. Babylon's supremacy lasted a little *more* than seventy years in the eastern part of her empire and a little *less* in the western part. The interval between her final defeat of Assyria and her own defeat by Persia was just about exactly seventy years. It can be seen, therefore, that there are good grounds for maintaining that Jeremiah's prophecy of the 'seventy years' was fulfilled both literally and accurately. But even if we regard the number seventy as an approximate or 'round' figure, we should note that it is still a *literal* seventy — not merely a symbolical seventy.

4. *This* (the fourth point which we noted concerning Jeremiah's prophecies) is the reason why Daniel made his great prayer to God. *God had promised that He would cause the Jews to return to their land after the seventy years ended.* Daniel had 'perceived in the books the number of years . . . namely, seventy years' in the first year of Darius the Mede. That is, in 538 B.C., shortly after the completion of the seventy years. Daniel was pleading with God to remember His promise and to fulfil it. He was pleading with God to let the Jews return to their land and rebuild it.

God's response to Daniel's prayer

This is what we read next:

> 'While I was speaking and praying, confessing my sin and the sin of my people Israel, and presenting my supplication before the Lord my God for the holy hill of my God; while I was speaking in prayer, the man Gabriel, whom I had seen in the vision at the first, came to me in swift flight at the time of the evening sacrifice. He came and he said to me, "O Daniel, I have now come out to give you wisdom and understanding. At the beginning of your supplications a word went forth, and I have come to tell it to you, for you are greatly beloved; therefore consider the word and understand the vision . . ." ' (Daniel 9:20–23)

The R.V. translates verse 23 slightly differently: '*At the beginning of thy supplications the commandment went forth, and I am come to tell thee; for thou art greatly beloved; therefore consider the matter, and understand the vision.*' This translation gives a sense slightly different from that of the R.S.V. It seems to suggest that we have here an answer to Daniel's prayer — his prayer for the restoration of the temple and city of Jerusalem.

The 'commandment which went forth' may well be God's commandment that the Jews be allowed to return to their land and begin rebuilding. It can be seen that if this *is* the true meaning, God answered Daniel's request even before he made it. His action was as good as His word, for that very same year Cyrus issued his edict permitting the Jews to return to their land and rebuild the temple.

The seventy weeks

Gabriel continues,

> '*Seventy weeks of years are decreed concerning your people and your holy city, to finish the transgression, to put an end to sin, and to atone for iniquity, to bring in everlasting righteousness, to seal both vision and prophet, and to anoint a most holy place.*' (Daniel 9:24)

Daniel has been assured (if our interpretation of verse 23 is correct) that Jeremiah's prophecy has been fulfilled; but God now reveals another prophecy which yet again involves the number seventy – and again the prophecy concerns Jerusalem and the Jews.

Now critical scholars deny that this prophecy has anything (except in the vaguest sense) to do with Christ. They believe, quite simply, that it concerns the time of Antiochus Epiphanes. We shall consider this view further on in the chapter; but for the time being we shall proceed with our own interpretation.

Daniel is told that within 'seventy weeks' ('of years' is not in the original) sin will be atoned for and true righteousness will be brought in. This surely refers to the wonderful fact of Christ's atoning sacrifice on the cross, through which man may receive full forgiveness of sins and may be clothed with the righteousness of Christ. See Hebrews 9:15, 26; II Corinthians 5:19; Romans 3:21, 22.

Daniel is told also that within seventy weeks 'vision and prophet' will be sealed – indicating the end of the Old Testament form of divine revelation together with the institution of the prophets, and the coming to pass of the main event for which they were preparing. John the Baptist was the last of the prophets, and the event for which they were preparing was the coming of the Messianic kingdom of Heaven.

> 'The law and the prophets were until John; since then the good news of the kingdom of God is preached . . .' (Luke 16:16)

> 'Think not that I have come to abolish the law and the prophets; I have come not to abolish them but to fulfil them . . .' (Matthew 5:17)

Daniel learns also that within seventy weeks 'the most

holy' (R.V.) will be anointed. This surely refers to the anointing of the divine Messiah ('the anointed one'). Centuries later Gabriel (the messenger who is speaking to Daniel) tells Mary that 'the child to be born will be called holy, the Son of God' (Luke 1:35) and Jesus is later hailed as 'the Holy One of God' (Mark 1:24; John 6:69), this being one of the titles of the Messiah (Psalm 16:10; Acts 13:35—37). The early church spoke to God of 'thy *holy* servant Jesus, whom thou didst *anoint*' (Acts 4:27). On one occasion Jesus opened the book of Isaiah and read, 'The Spirit of the Lord is upon me, because he has *anointed* me to preach good news to the poor'. After He had finished reading He closed the book and said, 'Today this scripture has been fulfilled in your hearing' (Luke 4:18—21). We know also that Christ, the divine Messiah, has been anointed prophet, priest and king (Acts 3:20—24); Hebrews 1:8, 9; 5:4, 5, 10).

'Anoint the most holy' can also be understood to mean 'anoint a most holy *place*' (as in the R.S.V.), referring to the Holy of holies, the innermost sanctum of the tabernacle and temple, the place of meeting with God and itself therefore typical of Christ. Christ called His own body a temple (John 2:19—21) and John wrote, 'the Word became flesh, and tabernacled among us' (John 1:14, R.V. mg.). God came down and dwelt among men in a 'tabernacle' or 'temple' of flesh. As the old tabernacle was anointed at the beginning (Exodus 40:9), so Christ was anointed as the new Tabernacle and Temple which superceded the tabernacle and temples of the Old Covenant. Now that He is no longer living among us in the flesh, we (those who have accepted Him as Saviour and Lord) are His temple and He dwells in us by His Holy Spirit (I Corinthians 3:16).

Daniel is told that all these things will be accomplished within 'seventy weeks'. Now the word translated 'week' literally means 'seven' and can, in the Bible, mean a seven of days or a seven of years (see Genesis 29:27, 28). In this case it is likely, as the R.S.V. assumes, that weeks of years are meant. If this is so, we are told that 490 years (70 x 7) are decreed upon the Jews and upon Jerusalem. Within this time sin will be atoned for, everlasting righteousness will be brought in, vision and prophet will be sealed and the Most Holy will be anointed. We have seen that in fact all these things had been done by the time Christ finished His work on earth some two thousand years ago.

We take the 'seventy weeks' to mean a literal period of 490 years, and there are at least three good reasons why we should do so. Firstly, Daniel 9 is of a generally literal, straightforward nature — it does not contain the symbolism and imagery of the earlier visions. Secondly, if Jeremiah's prophecy of the 'seventy years' was fulfilled literally, it is extremely likely that Daniel's prophecy of the 'seventy weeks' was also fulfilled literally. And thirdly, it can be shown that the prophecy of the seventy weeks *was* fulfilled literally!

The commandment to restore and to build Jerusalem

Gabriel continues,

> *'Know therefore and discern, that from the going forth of the commandment to restore and to build Jerusalem unto the anointed one, the prince, shall be seven weeks, and threescore and two weeks: it shall be built again, with street and moat, even in troublous times.'* (Daniel 9:25, R.V.)[1]

We learn now that the seventy weeks are dated from 'the going forth of the commandment to restore and to build Jerusalem'. The immediate question is, 'When did this commandment go forth?'. To answer this question we shall have to consider just how the Jews returned and how they rebuilt Jerusalem.

These events took place in two main stages. In the first stage a large group of Jews returned under the leadership of Sheshbazzar and Zerubbabel, probably in 537 B.C. They had specific permission from Cyrus to build the temple in Jerusalem; but more than this, we read that those who returned were those 'whose spirit God had stirred to go up to rebuild the house of the Lord which is in Jerusalem' (Ezra 1: 5). It was *God's* desire and command that they should rebuild the temple. They commenced building the temple the year

1. Various punctuation arrangements are possilbe in 9:25. We have followed that of A.V., R.V. margin and N.I.V., as this seems to fit the historical facts best.

after their return and finally completed it twenty years later, just over seventy years after Nebuchadnezzar destroyed the first temple. There is no evidence that they tried to rebuild the city itself.

In the second stage, another group of Jews returned to Jerusalem some eighty years later, led by Ezra. The return took place in 458 B.C., the seventh year of the reign of Artaxerxes Longimanus, the exiles arriving in Jerusalem towards the end of July. There is considerable controversy over the date of Ezra's return to Jerusalem, and this controversy will be referred to later. But for the time being, we shall assume that as the Bible says, he returned in the seventh year of Artaxerxes I (Ezra 7:7). Ezra carried with him a letter from Artaxerxes which gave him authority to organise the colony in Judah according to Hebrew law and to obtain and carry money and material for the beautification and service of the temple. He did not carry any specific permission to rebuild the city of Jerusalem, but it is apparent from Ezra 4:7–23 that he did in fact begin to do this. In this passage we learn that the enemies of the Jews sent a letter to Artaxerxes, saying,

> '. . . be it known to the king that the Jews who came up from you to us have gone to Jerusalem. They are rebuilding that rebellious and wicked city; they are finishing the walls and repairing the foundations. Now be it known to the king that, if this city is rebuilt and the walls finished, they will not pay tribute, custom, or toll, and the royal revenue will be impaired.' (Ezra 4:12, 13)

Who were these 'Jews who came up from Artaxerxes'? It is clear that they must have come to Jerusalem *before* the coming of Nehemiah — and the only such group we know of is *the group led by Ezra in the seventh year of the reign of Artaxerxes*. It would appear therefore that the rebuilding of Jerusalem was initiated *by Ezra*.

The writers of the letter (Samaritans and others) went on to claim that Jerusalem had been a rebellious city in the past and therefore it was not safe to allow the Jews to rebuild it. Artaxerxes was convinced by the argument and gave orders that the building should cease. We read that the Samaritans & Co. 'went in haste to the Jews at Jerusalem and by force and power made them cease'. The Samaritans did not have much difficulty in getting Artaxerxes to forbid the rebuilding; and this supports the idea that Ezra's group of Jews were the builders, because even though they had 'come up from' Artaxerxes, they did not have any specific permission to rebuild the city.[2]

We have further evidence that Ezra began to rebuild Jerusalem in a prayer he made to God about four months after his arrival.

> '. . . God hath not forsaken us in our bondage, but hath extended mercy unto us in the sight of the kings of Persia, to give us a reviving, to set up the house of our God, and to repair the ruins thereof, and to give us a wall in Judah and in Jerusalem.' (Ezra 9:9, R.V.)

The immediate question is, what did Ezra mean by a 'wall in Jerusalem'? He did not mean just the city wall, as he would have used a different word for that. In this case 'wall' translates *gader,* which is also translated elsewhere as 'fence'. It refers primarily to the sort of protective wall which, for example, surrounds a vineyard. The idea, as indicated in the R.S.V. translation, is that of *protection.* When God 'gave a wall in Jerusalem' He made Jerusalem capable of protecting the Jews. Ezra was obviously speaking of the literal city of Jerusalem, as in the same verse he had just spoken of the literal temple. A Jerusalem capable of protecting the Jews was a Jerusalem which had been *rebuilt.* And Ezra was not talking just about the city wall; he was talking about *the entire city.* We understand the actual word 'wall' in a metaphorical sense, but it implies the literal rebuilding of Jerusalem. This indicates that *Ezra was at least planning to rebuild Jerusalem.* The passage quoted earlier from Ezra 4 seems to show that in fact he did begin this task.

The Jews with Ezra probably began by building within the city, and they started on the wall only at a later stage, nearer

2. It should be noted that chronologically verses 7—23 do not belong to the fourth chapter of Ezra. They should come later in the book, but are included in this chapter as an example of opposition to the Jews from neighbouring enemies. They are in Aramaic from verse 8, and are regarded as particularly reliable by critical scholars.

the time of Nehemiah. It was then that the Samaritans began
to cause trouble. They caused the rebuilding to cease 'by
force and power' — and this would obviously include the
breaking down of the offending wall. It is probable that this
was the news that distressed Nehemiah so much in the
twentieth year of Artaxerxes, thirteen years after Ezra's
arrival in Jerusalem. He was at Susa, in Persia, when he met
some Jews from Judah and asked them how Jerusalem and the
people of Judah were faring. They replied that the people
were in great trouble and that 'the wall of Jerusalem is broken
down, and its gates are destroyed by fire' (Nehemiah 1:1—4).
Nehemiah quickly obtained permission from Artaxerxes to
rebuild the wall, and so came to Jerusalem.

When he arrived there, he found there were only a few
people living in the city, and that 'the houses were not
builded' (7:4, R.V.). Nehemiah 7:3, however, states clearly
that there were people living in Jerusalem in their own
houses — which does indicate that *some* houses had been
built. The rebuilding of the whole city was a task which must
have taken many years to complete; so it is not surprising
that much work remained to be done. It is likely, furthermore,
just as a previous generation had been slow to begin work on
the temple. They needed a man like Nehemiah to come and
chivvy them on, and this is precisely what he did. He exhorted
them to rebuild the wall, and despite intense opposition from
neighbouring enemies, it was repaired in fifty-two days. Ezra
was then called upon to read the Law and the people pledged
themselves to observe its commands.

The temple or the city?

Having said all this, we are in a better position to answer our
question, 'When did the commandment to restore and to build
Jerusalem go forth?'.

The first point we need to consider is this. Did the commandment go forth during the reign of Cyrus, when the Jews
began rebuilding the temple? Or was it during the reign of
Artaxerxes I, when they began rebuilding the city? Does the
rebuilding of 'Jerusalem' include the rebuilding of the *temple*,
or does it mean the later rebuilding of the *city*?

We can answer that the commandment of verse 25 *could*

refer to Cyrus's edict (or rather the commandment of God which caused it) — but not necessarily. The revelation of Daniel 9 was given in response to a prayer made by Daniel. He had prayed, 'Cause thy face to shine upon thy *sanctuary,* which is desolate . . . behold our desolations, and the *city* which is called by thy name' (vv. 17, 18). Daniel first asked restoration of the *city.* As Daniel made two requests, so God may have given two answers. The first was, we suggest, the commandment of verse 23 — given in immediate response to Daniel's prayer — the commandment to build the temple. The second was the commandment of verse 25 — then future — the commandment to build the city. As God gave two commandments, so the temple and city were rebuilt in two stages. A group of Jews returned during the reign of Cyrus and rebuilt the *temple.* A second group returned during the reign of Artaxerxes and began rebuilding the *city.*

Daniel does draw a distinction between the temple and the city of Jerusalem, so it is certainly possible, if not probable, that the rebuilding of 'Jerusalem' refers to the rebuilding of the *city* which began during the reign of Artaxerxes. It is significant that the seventy weeks are decreed concerning the people and *the city* (9:24) — powerful evidence that the seventy weeks are indeed to be dated from the commandment to rebuild the city.

Ezra or Nehemiah?

So much for the 'temple' versus the 'city'. We shall now try to show that the commandment to restore and build Jerusalem is to be associated with the coming of Ezra, rather than that of Nehemiah. We have shown already that the Jews began rebuilding the city of Jerusalem *before* Nehemiah's arrival, and that there is good reason to believe that Nehemiah's work was simply a continuation of Ezra's work.

It should be noted that right from the beginning, Nehemiah was in absolutely no doubt that the wall of Jerusalem should be rebuilt immediately. In fact it seems that he was shocked and distressed to hear that it had not been built already. This suggests that as far as Nehemiah was concerned, God's commandment had gone forth already.

Now the seventy weeks are decreed concerning the *people*

and the *city* (9:24). This suggests that they are to be dated from the reorganisation of the *people* and the rebuilding of the *city* by Ezra when he returned in the seventh year of Artaxerxes. We can say truthfully that *the spiritual and physical rebuilding of the nation began with the return of Ezra.* Apart from the building of the temple, very little seems to have been achieved by the first group of returned exiles — Jerusalem continued to lie in ruins, and both spiritually and physically the people remained at an extremely low ebb. As John Bright says in his book, *A History of Israel,* Ezra emerged as a figure of 'towering importance' who came to be regarded as 'no less than a second Moses'. 'If Moses was Israel's founder, it was Ezra who reconstituted Israel and gave her faith a form in which it could survive through the centuries.'[3] The post-exilic theocracy was a new phase in the history of Israel. It began with the work of Ezra and ended (as far as God was concerned) with the work of Christ. We shall see shortly that *this phase of Israel's history lasted precisely 490 years (seventy weeks).*

As we have shown, the Bible implies very strongly indeed that Ezra not only reconstituted the religious life of the people, but he also initiated the rebuilding of the city of Jerusalem. It is the only solution which fits all the facts we are given. *The very earliest work of rebuilding the city (as opposed to the temple) that the Old Testament speaks of is the work of rebuilding recorded in Ezra 4:7–23.* The Old Testament clearly indicates that the purposeful rebuilding of the city was initiated by a group of Jews that 'came up from Artaxerxes' before Nehemiah. The only such group that the Old Testament knows of is the band of Jews led by Ezra in the seventh year of the reign of Artaxerxes I.

It is in fact almost universally accepted by both conservative and critical scholars that the Jews began rebuilding the city of Jerusalem during the reign of Artaxerxes Longimanus, before the arrival of Nehemiah, as described in Ezra 4:7–23. Critical scholars actually consider this section to be particularly authentic and reliable. The present writer even remembers reading in one critical commentary that the author or editor of the book of Ezra may have 'confused' Ezra's return with

3. *A History of Israel,* by John Bright (S.C.M. Press, 1960) p. 374.

that of the Jews mentioned in Ezra 4:12. Many critical scholars believe the Biblical date of Ezra's return to be erroneous (they believe that he came to Jerusalem after Nehemiah); but the aforesaid commentary does at least imply that *some* Jews did return to Jerusalem around 458 B.C., and began rebuilding the city. As for conservative opinion, suffice it to quote a sample from *The New Bible Commentary Revised,* Inter-Varsity Press (p. 401). Ezra 4:12 'is highly important evidence for a migration of Jews in the reign of Artaxerxes. If the traditional dating of Ezra's return (c. 458 B.C.) be accepted, the verse could well indicate the group which returned with him. The cessation of the building, which was unauthorised, may have been that reported to Nehemiah (Nehemiah 1:1 ff.). Ezra may have realised that no effective reform could be achieved without the security of a wall, but he had no commission for this, hence the appeal to Nehemiah. Apart from this reconstruction, there is no historically-attested connection for this group.'

It should be mentioned again that certain scholars do not accept that Ezra returned in the seventh year of Artaxerxes I. In fact a very good case can be made out for the Biblical chronology; but as it happens, this controversy is largely irrelevant to our discussion. We are trying to show that *the Bible* predicted the date of Christ's arrival. We are therefore concerned with the *Biblical* date of Ezra's return. However, it is worth quoting here a point made by *The New Bible Commentary Revised* (p. 397). '. . . the Chronicler was so close to Ezra and Nehemiah, even allowing a date as late as c. 350 B.C., that a major chronological blunder is unlikely. Indeed, the view that Ezra himself was the Chronicler is maintained by W. F. Albright and other leading scholars.'

To say that the Chronicler could have got such an important historical fact wrong is rather like saying that a modern historian could be confused over whether Queen Victoria reigned before or after Edward VII. The ingenious but inconclusive arguments against Ezra coming to Jerusalem before Nehemiah are all completely overshadowed by the simple fact that *an authority who was actually there at the time (or at least very soon afterwards) says that Ezra did come first.*

But we are digressing. The question we need to ask is not 'When did the Jews begin to rebuild Jerusalem?'. It is 'When did the *commandment* to rebuild go forth?'. We read in Ezra 7:6 that Artaxerxes 'granted Ezra all that he asked, for the hand of the Lord his God was upon him'. Since Ezra was not given specific permission to rebuild Jerusalem and cannot therefore have asked for it, we can take it that when Ezra left for Jerusalem, the commandment for its restoration had not yet 'gone forth' from God. We are told that in the days immediately following the exiles' arrival in late July, they 'aided the people and the *house of God*' (Ezra 8:36). As there is no mention of the city here, we can take it that the commandment must have 'gone forth' some time *after* July, 458 B.C.

Now the aforementioned prayer of Ezra is the only indication we have as to when the commandment did go forth. In the prayer he says that God has extended mercy to the Jews in the sight of the kings of Persia in order 'to give us a reviving, to set up the house of our God, and to repair the ruins thereof, and to give us a wall in Judah and in Jerusalem'. *Ezra clearly believed that it was God's will that Jerusalem should be rebuilt.* Furthermore, he did not speak of the rebuilding as something to come in the future — he spoke of it as something which was, or could be, just as much a present reality as the restoration of the temple.

This is the first time since Daniel that such a statement occurs. Hitherto it has always been the restoration of the temple only. Zechariah 1:16 (written in 520 B.C.) does mention Jerusalem together with the temple, but only in such a way as to confirm that the commandment to rebuild Jerusalem had not yet gone forth.[4] The command to rebuild the temple was, at that time, very emphatic. By contrast, the clearest reference to the building of the city (Zechariah 1:16) was guarded and somewhat vague — a promise of something to come in the future. Something to look forward to. Ezra's

---

4. Zechariah 2:1–5 is even less specific than 1:16. It should be mentioned that some critical scholars believe that passages in Isaiah which refer to the rebuilding of Jerusalem were written as late as about 520 B.C. Likewise, passages involving Cyrus are thought by many to have been written around 545 B.C. The Biblical view (as in John 12:38) seems to be that the whole book was written by Isaiah — who lived long before the time of Daniel.

words were much more definite. He clearly believed that God had brought the Jews back to build both the temple and the city of Jerusalem.

It is probable, therefore, that when Ezra prayed this prayer, he had already received the 'go-ahead' from God to rebuild Jerusalem. Doubtless this 'go-ahead' took the form of a deep conviction laid on his heart. It is not difficult to imagine this happening soon after his arrival in Jerusalem — still in ruins eighty years after Cyrus's edict. In fact is is quite possible that when Ezra prayed this prayer, he had already exhorted the Jews to begin rebuilding.

The New Bible Commentary Revised doubts if the building of the wall could have begun so soon after his return. But as explained already, Ezra was not just speaking of the wall — he was speaking of the whole city. There is no reason why some building work within the city (as opposed to the wall) could not have begun at that time. Ezra 4:12, 13 does indicate that the Jews began building both the city and its wall. As mentioned earlier, they probably began by building within the city, and started on the walls only at a later stage, nearer the time of Nehemiah. It was then that the Samaritans began to cause trouble.

However, whether or not the Jews had begun the actual work of rebuilding when Ezra prayed his prayer, there is good reason to believe that the *commandment* to build had gone forth (from God). And this is what really matters. The fact that only a few houses were built and that the work came to a temporary halt need not worry. us. It was a fulfilment of Daniel's prophecy that the city would be built in 'a troubled time' (9:25), and the Bible compares it with the way in which the building of the temple was delayed also (Ezra 4—6). We need to remember that very little was done about the building of the temple until about eighteen years after Cyrus's edict. In both cases, it would appear, there was a considerable lapse of time between the 'going forth' of God's commandment and an effective response to that commandment. Just as the building of the temple needed the impetus given by Haggai and Zechariah, so the building of the city needed the impetus given by Nehemiah.

Ezra's prayer was made in early December or late November

(see Ezra 10); so we can take it that the commandment to restore and build Jerusalem went forth sometime *during the months August to November, 458 B.C.* This, the present writer believes, is the answer the Old Testament supplies to the question 'When did the commandment to restore and to build Jerusalem go forth?'. The answer has to be looked for; but it is there — 'seek, and you will find; knock, and it will be opened to you'.

The Messiah

Daniel is told that 'unto the anointed one (Messiah), the prince' shall be 69 weeks (7 weeks plus 62 weeks). That is, the Messiah will appear 483 years (7 x 69) from the latter part of the year 458 B.C. Remembering that there was no year 0, this brings us to the latter part of the year 26 A.D. *It was about this very time that Jesus Christ began His public ministry.* It is very highly probable from astronomical calculations that Christ was crucified on 7th April, 30 A.D.[5] It is apparent that His public ministry extended over a period of two to four years, three and a half years being one of the calculated possibilities. We shall see in a few moments that the prophecy of Daniel 9 indicates that it did last exactly three and a half years — and this is in fact the traditional span. (In our final chapter we shall see that evidence for this can be found in the eleventh chapter of Revelation.) If we count back three and a half years from 7th April, 30 A.D., we come to the month of October, 26 A.D. This month is in the latter part (August–November) of the year 26 A.D., *the very time predicted by Daniel's prophecy.* It has been calculated from other evidence too that 26 A.D. is the most likely date for the beginning of Jesus's public ministry (see chapter 7 of *New Testament Times,* by Merrill C. Tenney).

Now it is true that the date of the commandment to rebuild Jerusalem is not immediately obvious. Reasons can be found for identifying it with the year 458 B.C., and other reasons can be found for 538 or 445 B.C. The picture is further obscured by uncertainty over the correct punctuation

5.   See Merrill C. Tenney, *New Testament Times* (Inter-Varsity Press, 1967), chapter 7.

in verse 25 (we have used the punctuation of A.V., R.V. margin and N.I.V.). The answer is not laid on a plate before us. It is partially hidden, and we have to search for it. But as we said in our introductory chapter, all Daniel's prophecies are something of a riddle, and one gets the impression that God made it this way deliberately. The ambiguity may well be intentional.

Because the correct answer to our problem is not crystal clear at the first glance, and because there has been so much disagreement and confusion over this prediction, there are many who declare that it is wrong to look for an exact interpretation. The New Testament plainly indicates, however, that the Old Testament Messianic prophecies were *not* crystal clear in meaning. Jesus often had to explain them before the disciples understood them. Note also that although Jesus specifically told His disciples that we cannot know the date of the *second* advent, He said no such thing with regard to the *first* advent. Rather, He repeatedly showed them that His first advent had been predicted in great detail by the Old Testament scriptures.

With regard to Daniel's prophecy of the seventy weeks, we are plainly told that there were to be sixty-nine weeks (if we follow the A.V., R.V. mg. and N.I.V. punctuation in verse 25) from the going forth of the commandment to rebuild Jerusalem to the coming of 'an anointed one, a prince'. We are also told that after the sixty-nine weeks (whichever punctuation we use), 'an anointed one' would be cut off. Ezra 4:7—23 and 7:7 and 9:9 imply very strongly indeed that the rebuilding of the city of Jerusalem was initiated by Ezra. And it is an irrefutable fact that there were exactly 483 years (69 weeks) between the Biblical date of Ezra's coming to Jerusalem and 26 A.D., the year in which Jesus Christ, the Messiah, probably began His public ministry. Some prefer to think that this is pure coincidence. To the present writer, a 'coincidence' of this magnitude is so unlikely as to be totally out of the question. It is more reasonable to accept it, partially hidden though it is, as a prediction of the date of Christ's coming.

There are some who maintain that if the date of Christ's coming had really been predicted in this remarkable way, it would have been mentioned in the New Testament. It is true that the 'seventy weeks' are not specifically mentioned, but there can be no doubt that as far as the New Testament is concerned, the prophecy as a whole applies to the time of Christ. This is particularly true of verse 24. Also, on the occasion when Jesus mentioned Daniel by name (Matthew 24: 15–21; Mark 13:14–19; Luke 21:20–24), He appeared to link Daniel 9:27 with the destruction of Jerusalem in 70 A.D. – indicating in a very specific way that 9:24–27 *does* look beyond Antiochus to the time of Christ.

Maybe Christ said a lot more about Daniel after His resurrection, when He showed His disciples 'the things concerning himself in all the scriptures'. Maybe Paul and others did point to this prophecy when they 'argued from the scriptures' to prove that Jesus was the Christ. But perhaps this particular gem of prophecy was left for people of a later age to discover – people who would possess fuller historical information, and for whom exact dates and lengths of time might therefore be more meaningful.

Other conservative views

What about the other explanations of the 'seventy weeks' which one finds in conservative commentaries?

Some conservative scholars believe that the seventy weeks should be dated from the edict of Cyrus. They believe that the prophecy points to Christ; but they have to maintain that the seventy weeks are only symbolical. This is because 490 years from 538 B.C. brings us up to only 48 B.C. But as we have explained already, there are strong reasons for believing that the seventy weeks are meant to be taken literally.

Other conservatives date the seventy weeks from Nehemiah's commission in 445 B.C. This brings us up to 46 A.D. for the end of the seventy weeks, and 39 A.D. for the appearance of the 'anointed one'. This is certainly much closer to the time of Christ, but it is still not an exact fulfilment. One way of getting round this is to calculate in 'prophetic' years of 360 days each. This brings us up to 32 A.D. for the appearance of the 'anointed one'; but it is not a satisfactory solution. Calculating in 'prophetic' years is too much of a 'wangle', and in any case it is now almost certain that Jesus was crucified in 30 A.D. Thus many conservatives believe that the seventy weeks date from 445 B.C., but that the 'seventy' is only an approximate or round figure — albeit a literal one.

Perhaps the right way to view the problem is to accept that the 'symbolical' interpretation is correct as far as it goes. But beneath the surface there is 'hidden treasure' — namely, the prediction that Christ would appear in 26 A.D.

The fact that there are 483 years between 458 B.C. and 26 A.D. has been noticed before;[6] but strangely enough, very little has been made of this fact (so far as the present writer is aware). It provides a fulfilment which is both accurate and literal — not only satisfying and convincing in itself, but also consistent with the accurate, literal fulfilment of the prophecy of the 'seventy years'. Babylon was given literally seventy years, and Jerusalem was given literally seven times seventy years!

The first seven weeks

It remains to be asked, 'Why are the first sixty-nine weeks divided into a period of seven weeks, followed by a period of sixty-two weeks?'.

The most likely answer — and this is not difficult to see if we follow the A.V. and R.V. margin punctuation — is that it took forty-nine years (seven weeks) to build the city of Jerusalem.

> '. . . *from the going forth of the commandment to restore and to build Jerusalem unto the anointed one, the prince, shall be seven weeks, and threescore and two weeks: it shall be built again, with street and moat, even in troublous times.' (Daniel 9:25)*

An apt description of the difficulties Ezra and Nehemiah had to contend with!

The seventieth week

> '*And after the sixty-two weeks, an anointed one shall be cut off, and shall have nothing; and the people of the prince who is to come shall destroy the city and the sanctuary.*

6. See *The Westminster Dictionary of the Bible* (1944), p.128.

*Its end shall come with a flood, and to the end there shall
be war; desolations are decreed. And he shall make a strong
covenant with many for one week; and for half of the week[7]
he shall cause sacrifice and offering to cease; and upon the
wing of abominations shall come one who makes desolate,
until the decreed end is poured out on the desolator.'
(Daniel 9:26, 27)*

We have learned that the Messiah will appear sixty-nine
weeks (seven weeks plus sixty-two weeks) after the going
forth of the commandment to rebuild Jerusalem. We are now
told, in verse 26, that some time after His appearance the
Messiah will be 'cut off' and will 'have nothing', indicating
that He will be killed, perhaps in the prime of His life, and
that He will be utterly forsaken and desolate, certainly not
having the earthly kingdom expected by the Jews. In verse 27
we are told that following His manifestation, the Messiah
will 'make a strong covenant with many' for the space of
seven years (one week). In the middle of this period He will
bring to an end the Old Covenant system of sacrifices.

Daniel does not specify directly whether the one who makes
the covenant is the 'anointed one' or the destroying 'prince
who is to come'. Nevertheless, it is highly probable that the
'he' of verse 27 refers back to the 'anointed one', since He is
the principal character in verse 26. (The word 'prince' takes
a subordinate position in the verse). Also, Daniel goes on in
verse 27 to speak of a desolating 'one who shall come', who
seems to be a different person from the one who makes the
covenant. It is reasonable to assume, therefore, that the one
who makes the covenant is the 'anointed one', and the 'one
who shall come' is the 'prince who is to come'.

So let us now try to identify this period of seven years
during which the Messiah 'shall make a strong covenant with
many' — better translated, 'establish a covenant' or 'cause a
covenant to prevail'.

The beginning of the period is marked by His appearance —
'unto Messiah, the prince, shall be sixty-nine weeks' (see R.V.
margin). This, surely, is the time of Christ's baptism by John,
when He was recognised to be both Messiah and King of
Israel, and His public life began (John 1:29—49; Luke 3:23;

---

7.   Or 'in the middle of the week', as in R.V. margin.

16:16; Acts 10:36, 37). When Jesus came to be baptised, He
was 'anointed' with the Holy Spirit. This event marked the
beginning of His public life. It was entirely appropriate that
the appearance of the Messiah ('the anointed one') should be
marked by His actual anointing. Moreover, at the very moment
of anointing God revealed Jesus's Messiahship with these words
spoken out of Heaven: 'Thou art my beloved Son; with thee
I am well pleased' (Mark 1:11; cf. Psalms 2:7; Isaiah 42:1).

In his book *Baptism in the Holy Spirit,* James Dunn shows
that the anointing of Jesus by the Holy Spirit at the time of
His baptism was an event of enormous importance (see chapter
3, 'The Experience of Jesus at Jordan'). Dunn shows that for
Jesus it marked the actual point in time at which the Old
Covenant age ended and the new, Messianic age began.

From the very beginning of His ministry, Jesus preached
about the kingdom of God — 'The time is fulfilled, and the
kingdom of God is at hand' (Mark 1:15). And the outcome of
His ministry was the establishing of a 'New Covenant'
(Jeremiah 31:31–34); Luke 22:20). Compare 'he shall make a
strong covenant with many' (Daniel 9:27) with 'this is my
blood of the covenant, which is poured out for many'
(Matthew 26:28).

The event marking the end of this seven-year period during
which Christ 'established the covenant' is rather more difficult
to identify; but the following solution meets every require-
ment.

Paul, the last chosen of the apostles, wrote,

'Last of all, as to one untimely born, he appeared also to
me.' (I Corinthians 15:8)

'For I would have you know, brethren, that the gospel which
was preached by me is not man's gospel. For I did not
receive it from man, nor was I taught it, but it came
through a revelation of Jesus Christ.' (Galatians 1:11, 12)

Paul was apparently the last individual to whom Christ
appeared in person, and it was to Paul that the gospel of the
New Covenant was revealed in its most complete form. Paul
was the last of the apostles to be commissioned by Jesus —
the apostles being a select band of disciples to whom Christ
specially entrusted His message of the New Covenant. In a very

striking way, therefore, Paul's commissioning marked the end
of Christ's work of 'establishing' the New Covenant. It is
very possible that Paul received his revelation and commission
from Christ three and a half years after His crucifixion and
seven years after the commencement of His ministry on
earth; so this event could well mark the end of the seventieth
'week' during which He 'made a strong covenant with many'.

This is particularly appropriate, because Daniel is told,
'Seventy weeks are decreed upon thy people and upon thy
holy city' (R.V.). The idea conveyed is one of *judgment* —
the Jews and their city have only seventy weeks to go! It was
to Paul that Christ finally made it clear that 'there is no
distinction between Jew and Greek' (Romans 10:12) — in
other words, *the Jews were no longer the special chosen
people of God and Jerusalem was no longer the special place
for the worship of God.* Paul was the apostle specially commissioned by Christ to take the gospel to the Gentiles after
it had been rejected by the Jews.[8]

Let us look at one of Jesus's parables.

> 'And he told this parable: "A man had a fig tree planted in
> his vineyard; and he came seeking fruit on it and found
> none. And he said to the vine-dresser, 'Lo, these three
> years I have come seeking fruit on this fig tree, and I find
> none. Cut it down; why should it use up the ground?' And
> he answered him, 'Let it alone, sir, this year also, till I dig
> about it and put on manure. And if it bears fruit next year,
> well and good; but if not, you can cut it down.' " ' (Luke
> 13:6–9)

The context, together with Hosea 9:10 and Joel 1:7, makes
it quite certain that the fig tree represents the Jewish nation.
Now this nation was the chosen people of God from the time
of the covenant made with Abraham until around the time of
Paul's commissioning as apostle to the Gentiles. According to
the parable, this period of time was divided into two parts.
The first part was three times as long as the second, and this
latter part was a time during which God gave the Jews 'one
more chance'. It might be thought that to take these relative

8.   Matthew 21:42, 43; Acts 13:44–48; 22:21; 26:17; 28:23–28;
     Romans 11:7–15; Galatians 1:16; 2:8; Ephesians 3:8; 1 Timothy
     2:7; II Timothy 4:17.

lengths of time literally is to read more into the parable than Christ intended. The fact remains, however, that the period during which the Jews were God's chosen people was divided in just this way. The parable indicates that God looked in vain for fruit during the first period. At the end of it He was almost prepared to cast the Jews off, but He relented and gave them one more chance. At the end of this second period He again looked for fruit, but finding none, He had to reject the Jews from being His chosen people.

Let us suppose that the 'seventy weeks' of the post-exilic theocracy was the 'one more chance' that God gave the Jews. This would make each of the 'years' of Jesus's parable to represent a period of 490 years, and would mean that the 'four years' started in 1928 B.C. *It was at about this very time that Abraham lived.* Abraham was the first member of the race which God singled out to be His chosen nation. It was from the time of Abraham that the Jews were God's peculiar people. But always they failed to produce the fruit He was looking for. About 1470 years (490 x 3) after the covenant with Abraham, God gave the Jews 'one more chance' when He re-made the nation under Ezra. But still they failed to produce the fruit He was looking for. And so it was that 490 years later, in 33 A.D., He had to cut down His fig tree — as predicted by Jesus.

> '. . . the kingdom of God will be taken away from you and given to a nation producing the fruits of it.' (Matthew 21: 43)

We have said that Paul's commissioning as apostle to the Gentiles marked the end of the period during which the Jews were God's chosen people. This is appropriate also because Paul typified this great change from one dispensation to another in his own life. He was a Pharisee of the Pharisees, a particularly fanatical believer in the Old Covenant and the privileges of the Jews. However, following his experience with Christ (an event which is given tremendous prominence in the New Testament),[9] the change was total and complete. Although retaining a great love for his people, he became the most vigorous preacher of the news that the Old Covenant has

9.   Acts 9:1—30; 22:3—21; 26:2—23; 1 Corinthians 9:1; 15:3—10; Galatians 1:11—2:9.

been superceded by the New, that there is now no distinction between Jew and Gentile. He sternly opposed all attempts to 'Judaise' Christianity. He was the first Christian really to understand that Gentiles do not have to become Jews in order to be members of God's family and that it is possible and desirable for Christians to abandon many of the observances which God required of the Jews under the Old Covenant.

Closely bound up with Paul's conversion and subsequent theology was the martyrdom of Stephen, an event which dramatically demonstrated the Jews' rejection of their Messiah. He had been brought before the Sanhedrin on charges of blasphemy and after surveying the history of Israel, he had attacked the Jews for continuing in the tradition of their fathers by killing the Messiah. This goaded the Jews to fury and when Stephen claimed to see Jesus standing at the right hand of God, they seized him and stoned him to death. Stephen's death resulted in a Jewish persecution, led by Paul, which scattered the Christians abroad. They preached the gospel wherever they went, but only to the Jews. It was not until after the time of Paul's conversion that it was preached to the Gentiles (Acts 11:19). Paul had been present at Stephen's martyrdom, and it was not so very long afterwards that Jesus met him and changed the course of his life and the role of the Jewish people in His dealings with mankind.

The first eight chapters of the book of Acts record the early preaching of the gospel to the Jewish nation. The narrative does not speak of any preaching to pure Gentiles. All were Jewish or partially Jewish by religion — including those converted at Pentecost, the Samaritans and the Ethiopian eunuch. Many individual Jews were converted, but the greater part of the nation rejected Christ. In the ninth chapter we read about Paul's conversion and his activities during the years immediately following that event. After this the narrative probably goes back a few years to tell the story of how Peter arrived at Joppa, where he was found by messengers from the Roman centurion Cornelius. We then read a long account of how Cornelius and his household were converted and how this event showed the church that Gentiles as well as Jews could become Christians. The narrative then goes on to describe the founding of a church of both Jews and Gentiles in Antioch. Because of his experience with Gentiles, Paul was eventually called upon to minister to this church. Up to the time of Paul's conversion, the book of Acts concentrates on the preaching of the gospel to the Jews. Following his conversion, the emphasis switches to the Gentiles.

Now Christ must have given Paul his teaching (with its special emphasis on the new relationship between Jew and Gentile) during the period following his conversion, possibly when he was in Arabia. The seventy weeks may therefore have ended some time after Paul's actual conversion. It could be that the exact point of time was marked by Cornelius's conversion. It was specially revealed to Peter at that time that the Gentiles were no longer 'unclean'. They and the Jews were now equal. The book of Acts represents this event as the opening of the door to the Gentiles. It is possible that Paul's basic theology was fully formed by this time (through special revelation); so it could be that he started preaching to the Gentiles at just about the same time as Peter. According to our caluclations, the seventy weeks ended in October, 33 A.D. It is very possible that the doors were opened to the Gentiles at just this time.

Merrill C. Tenney deals very well with New Testament chronology in his book *New Testament Times,* and the reader is advised to consult that book if he wishes to know how the various dates are worked out. In the chronological table at the end of Tenney's book, the following dates are given as the most probable in the light of the evidence we have at present. Opening of Jesus's ministry, 26 A.D. Crucifixion of Jesus, 30 A.D. Death of Stephen; conversion of Paul, 32/33 A.D. These dates agree precisely with the predictions of Daniel 9: 24—27.

To summarise, therefore, we suggest that the end of the seventy weeks was marked by 1. the completion of Christ's seven-year work of 'establishing' the New Covenant, and 2. the 'taking away of the kingdom of Heaven' from the Jewish nation and the opening of the door to the Gentiles.

The Crucifixion

As noted already, we are told that 'for half of (or 'in the

middle of') the week he (the Messiah) shall cause sacrifice and offering to cease'. 'Half' translates the Hebrew word *chatsi*, which does mean exactly a half. In other words, the Messiah will cause the sacrifice and the offering to cease three and a half years after the commencement of His ministry and half-way through the seven-year period during which He 'establishes the covenant'. We are also told, in the preceding verse, that some time after His appearance, the Messiah will be 'cut off' and will 'have nothing'. Christ's death on the cross is foretold here in the most dramatic and amazing way. We are told when He was to die, how He was to die and why He was to die.

Assuming He commenced His ministry in the latter part of the year 26 A.D., we are now told that He was to die three and a half years later in the early part of the year 30 A.D. As already stated, it is very probable that He did die in early 30 A.D., on 7th April. The Jews would have liked their Messiah to conquer all their earthly enemies and rule the world in omnipotent power from Jerusalem. His reign, they hoped and expected, would be both earthly and everlasting. This prophecy predicted not only that He would die, but that His death would be both abrupt and violent. And in His death He would apparently have nothing — certainly not the kingdom they hoped for. Indeed, while He was on the cross, Jesus did have nothing. Even His Father in Heaven 'forsook' Him.

And now, the reason for and the meaning of His death. The writer of the epistle to the Hebrews explains (Hebrews 9:1 — 10:22) that the sacrifices of the Old Covenant were, in themselves, quite ineffective. They were merely pictures or types of Christ's sacrifice on the cross. By His own sacrifice, 'once offered', Christ abolished and brought to an end the whole Old Covenant system of sacrifices and offerings. They had served their purpose as a temporary substitute and preparation for Christ's perfect and all-sufficient sacrifice; but there was now no further need for them, as signified by the curtain or 'veil' of the temple being 'torn in two, from top to bottom' (Matthew 27:51). Christ's atoning work on the cross is absolutely central to the message of the New Covenant — and this, perhaps, is why He arranged for His crucifixion to occur in the exact middle of the period during which He established the New Covenant.

The wording of Daniel 9:24—27 echoes Isaiah 53, suggesting that the suffering Servant of that chapter is indeed the Messiah, the Anointed One — 'He was despised and rejected by men . . . he was cut off out of the land of the living . . . he makes himself an offering for sin . . . by his knowledge shall the righteous one, my servant, make many to be accounted righteous'.

The destruction of Jerusalem

'And after the sixty-two weeks, an anointed one shall be cut off, and shall have nothing; and the people of the prince who is to come shall destroy the city and the sanctuary. Its end shall come with a flood, and to the end there shall be war; desolations are decreed. And he shall make a strong covenant with many for one week; and for half of the week he shall cause sacrifice and offering to cease; and upon the wing of abominations shall come one who makes desolate, until the decreed end is poured out on the desolator.'[10] (Daniel 9:26, 27)

Although in God's eyes the Old Covenant system of sacrifices came to an end on the day that Christ was crucified, the outward ritual of sacrifice was not finally discontinued until 70 A.D., when the Roman general Titus terminated the Jewish War with the siege and destruction of Jerusalem. It would seem that by this event God was visibly demonstrating the fact that the Old Covenant had come to an end — the Jews were no longer His special, chosen people and the temple at Jerusalem was no longer the special centre of worship — 'the hour is coming when neither on this mountain nor in Jerusalem will you worship the Father . . . the hour is coming, and now is, when the true worshippers will worship the Father in spirit and truth' (John 4:21—23).

Christ taught that the Jewish War was a fulfilment of prophecy (particularly Daniel's) and was God's punishment on the Jews for rejecting and murdering their divine Messiah, the Son of God.

'. . . he sent his son to them . . . And they took him . . . and killed him . . . When therefore the owner of the vine-

10.   Or 'the desolate', as in R.V. margin.

yard comes, what will he do to those tenants? ... He will put those wretches to a miserable death, and let out the vineyard to other tenants ... The very stone which the builders rejected has become the head of the corner ... the kingdom of God will be taken away from you and given to a nation producing the fruits of it.' (Matthew 21:37—43)

'The kingdom of heaven may be compared to a king who gave a marriage feast for his son, and sent his servants to call those who were invited to the marriage feast; but they would not come ... But they made light of it ... The king was angry, and he sent his troops and destroyed those murderers and burned their city ...' (Matthew 22:2—7)

'. . . you are the sons of those who murdered the prophets. Fill up, then, the measure of your fathers. You serpents, you brood of vipers, how are you to escape being sentenced to hell? . . . all this will come upon this generation. O Jerusalem, Jerusalem, killing the prophets and stoning those who are sent to you . . . Behold, your house is forsaken and desolate . . .' (Matthew 23:31—38)

'And when he drew near and saw the city he wept over it, saying, "Would that even today you knew the things that make for peace! But now they are hid from your eyes. For the days shall come upon you, when your enemies will cast up a bank about you and surround you, and hem you in on every side, and dash you to the ground, you and your children within you, and they will not leave one stone upon another in you; because you did not know the time of your visitation." ' (Luke 19:41—44)

'But when you see Jerusalem surrounded by armies, then know that its desolation has come near. Then let those who are in Judae flee to the mountains and let those who are inside the city depart, and let not those who are out in the country enter it; for these are days of vengeance, to fulfil all that is written . . . For great distress shall be upon the earth and wrath upon this people; they will fall by the edge of the sword, and be led captive among all nations; and Jerusalem will be trodden down by the Gentiles, until the times of the Gentiles are fulfilled.' (Luke 21:20—24)

'When therefore ye see the abomination of desolation,

which was spoken of by Daniel the prophet, standing in the holy place (let him that readeth understand), then let them that are in Judaea flee unto the mountains . . . for then shall be great tribulation, such as hath not been from the beginning of the world until now, no, nor ever shall be.' (Matthew 24:15—21, R.V.)

In Daniel 9:26, 27 it is prophesied that following the work of the Messiah, the people of a prince (the Roman soldiers under the command of Titus) will come and destroy the city and temple of Jerusalem. Its end shall come through a war characterised by a flood of blood, slaughter and desolation. The desolating Roman army will come 'upon the wing of abominations'. Thus up until the final pre-determined conclusion, God will pour out His wrath upon the desolated Jews and Jerusalem.

This is indeed a graphic description of the Jewish War and siege of Jerusalem. In addition to the terrible slaughter and destruction wrought by the Romans, the Jews themselves were slaughtering each other and perpetrating the most appalling abominations within Jerusalem and the temple itself. *And unlike Antiochus, the Romans utterly destroyed both the city and the temple of Jerusalem.*

Warning His disciples of the coming Jewish War and siege of Jerusalem, Jesus said, 'When therefore ye see the abomination of desolation, which was spoken of by Daniel the prophet, standing in the holy place (let him that readeth understand)' and 'when ye see Jerusalem compassed with armies, then know that her desolation is at hand. Then let them that are in Judaea flee unto the mountains' (Matthew 24:15; Luke 21:20; 21, R.V.). 'Let him that readeth understand', probably inserted by the writer of the gospel, suggests that the fulfilment of Daniel's prophecy was something within the experience and understanding of the early Christians. They escaped the horrors of the siege of Jerusalem, because they fled from Judaea before it took place, finding refuge in Pella, on the edge of the Arabian deserts. This strongly suggests that they took Christ's words as a warning of this event. The Jewish War was the pouring out of God's wrath on the Jews for their rejection of Christ; therefore it would have been entirely inappropriate for the Christians to have suffered with them.

It may be objected that the Jewish War does not fall within the seventy weeks. But then Daniel does not specifically say that it does. He says that Christ was crucified after the sixty-ninth week (verse 26a), in the middle of the seventieth week (verse 27a). This event was *followed* by the Jewish War (verses 26b and 27b) and it seems to be implied that the Jewish War was a direct *result* of the crucifixion. The Jewish War was, however, merely the outward and visible evidence of something which had already taken place several years before — the rejection of the Jews as God's special, chosen people. This final rejection took place at the end of the seventieth week ('seventy weeks are decreed upon thy people and upon thy holy city'). Christ witnessed to the Jews during His life-time; but they rejected Him and crucified Him. He continued to witness after His crucifixion and resurrection; but still they rejected Him. As Christ had predicted, their punishment was the loss of their privileged status.

> 'Jesus said to them, "Have you never read in the scrip-tures: 'The very stone which the builders rejected has be-come the head of the corner; this was the Lord's doing, and it is marvellous in our eyes'? Therefore I tell you, the kingdom of God will be taken away from you and given to a nation producing the fruits of it." ' (Matthew 21:42, 43)

Christ's herald, John the Baptist, had also warned the Jews that their punishment and the end of their privileges was near. (Luke 3:7—9)

Thus Christ 'established the covenant' for seven years (one week). Half-way through this period he was 'cut off', causing 'the sacrifice and the offering to cease'. Throughout this period the Jews rejected Him as the Messiah and so finally the Jews themselves were rejected from being God's special, chosen people.

The reader has probably noted that this interpretation indicates that verse 27 goes over much the same ground as verse 26. He may question why there should be this repetition. The reason is that verse 26 is a statement about a logical series of historical events. That is, the Messiah will be cut off and this will be followed by the destruction of Jerusalem. In verse 27, however, we are given the *meaning* of these historical events — i.e. the death of the Messiah is an essential part of

the establishing of the New Covenant and results in the cessation of the Old Covenant system of sacrifices.

The translation of the second part of the verse has caused
a great deal of difficulty and speculation. It indicates fairly
clearly that the resulting destruction of Jerusalem is God's
punishment (note the words 'decreed end' and read 'desolate'
rather than 'desolator', as in R.V. margin); but there is much
confusion over the meaning of *'upon the wing of abominations*
shall come one who makes desolate'. The R.S.V. accurately
translates *kanaph* as 'wing'. In fact here the word probably
means 'summit' or 'climax' but there may be some very good
reason for the choice of the particular word *kanaph,* primarily
meaning 'wing'. We must ask ourselves what picture it brings
to mind. Surely it suggests some great bird of prey coming
from afar and swooping down on its victim and tearing it to
pieces. This is precisely what the Roman army did — moreover,
its emblem was *the eagle!* We shall see that the 'abominations'
probably included the standards or ensigns of the Roman
armies. The 'one who makes desolate' must again be Titus,
'the prince who is to come'.

A piece of evidence in favour of this interpretation comes
from Deuteronomy 28, where God tells the people of Israel,
before they even enter the promised land and some 1200
years before Christ, that He will bless them if they keep His
commandments, but curse them if they do not keep them.
Daniel has already referred to this curse in his prayer (9:11).
In anticipation of the fact that they failed to keep His commandments, the curses occupy a good deal more space than
the blessings. Verses 49 to 68 are nothing less than a vivid
and accurate account of the siege of Jerusalem by the Romans
in 70 A.D. and the subsequent scattering and sufferings of the
Jewish people. The prophecy had a partial fulfilment in the
first siege and exile in the time of Nebuchadnezzar. But this
fulfilment was only partial. It was a warning which was dis-
regarded; so God had no alternative but to inflict His punishment to the full.

'The Lord will bring a nation against you from afar, from
the end of the earth, as swift as the eagle flies, a nation
whose language you do not understand, a nation of stern
countenance, who shall not regard the person of the old or

show favour to the young . . . They shall besiege you in all
your towns, until your high and fortified walls, in which
you trusted, come down throughout all your land . . . and
you shall eat the offspring of your own body, the flesh of
your sons and daughters, whom the Lord your God has
given you, in the siege and in the distress with which your
enemies shall distress you . . . and you shall be plucked off
the land which you are entering to take possession of it.
And the Lord will scatter you among all peoples, from one
end of the earth to the other . . . And among these nations
you shall find no ease, and there shall be no rest for the
sole of your foot; but the Lord will give you there a
trembling heart, and failing eyes, and a languishing soul;
your life shall hang in doubt before you; night and day you
shall be in dread, and have no assurance of your life.'
(Deuteronomy 28:49—66)

Here again we have the picture of a great bird of prey[11] coming
from afar and tearing its victim to pieces. No wonder Christ
wept over Jerusalem and told its people to weep for themselves rather than for Him!

Speaking of judgment and destruction falling upon ungodly
people, Jesus said, 'Where the body is, there the eagles will
be gathered together' (Luke 17:37). In Matthew's gospel (24:
28) these words are inserted at the end of a passage predicting the Jewish War of 70 A.D. (cf. Luke 21:20—24).

It seems clear, therefore, that the 'wing of abominations'
has something to do with the Roman armies. However, this is
probably not the full explanation, because 'wing' is in the
singular — not the plural. *Kanaph* is elsewhere translated as
'uttermost part, end, or corner (of the earth). — also 'skirt'
and 'border'. It gives the idea of some sort of *extremity*. This
would give the phrase the meaning of 'climax, summit or
pinnacle of abominations' — it suggests the absolute last word
in abominations. This is exactly what the Jews and their
religion represented after their rejection of Christ. On top of
all the abominations they had committed in the past (stoning
the prophets, etc.) they killed the Son of God. The religion
they then continued to practise became nothing less than a

11.   The Biblical 'eagle' is sometimes clearly the vulture.

mockery and an abomination to God. Further, Josephus tells us that during the Jewish War and siege of Jerusalem, the most appalling acts of horror and sacrilege were committed by the Jews within the temple itself. The Roman armies descended upon this pinnacle of abominations and punished it. It has also been suggested that the phrase refers to the pinnacle of the temple in which the Jews were practising their abominations and which the Romans destroyed.

The abomination of desolation

At this point let us see if we can identify 'the abomination of desolation, which was spoken of by Daniel the prophet' referred to by Jesus (Matthew 24:15, R.V.). The term 'abomination of desolation' is strongly reminiscent of Daniel 9:27, but it actually comes from 11:31 and 12:11, where the primary reference is to Antiochus's desecration of the temple in 167 B.C. (cf. I Maccabees 1:54). Jesus was indicating that there would be a *repetition* of this desecration.

There can be little doubt that Jesus was thinking primarily of the Jewish War which culminated in the siege and destruction of Jerusalem in 70 A.D. — as predicted in Daniel 9: 26, 27. He warns those of His disciples who are in Judaea to flee to the mountains when they see the abomination 'standing in the holy place'. In Mark 13:14, R.V., He says, 'standing where he ought not'. In Luke 21:20, 21 He says, 'when you see Jerusalem surrounded by armies, then know that its desolation has come near. Then let those who are in Judaea flee to the mountains . . . for these are days of vengeance, to fulfil all that is written'.

It seems that when Jesus spoke of the 'abomination of desolation', He was referring either to the desecration of the temple by the Jews, or to the presence on holy soil of the Roman armies — or possibly to both. The desecration of the temple by the Zealots in the winter of 67/68 A.D. was reminiscent of Antiochus Epiphanes' desecration of the temple in 167 B.C., and also it gave the Christians early warning of the coming catastrophe. On the other hand, the alien Romans were reminiscent of the alien Greeks, and the Christians could have guessed that they would desecrate the temple when they

saw them approaching the city. Also, Luke 21:20, 21 seems
to associate the abomination with Jerusalem being 'surrounded
by armies'. 'Standing in the holy place' need not necessarily
imply the temple. The R.V. marginal rendering is 'a holy
place'. The words could apply generally to the holy city of
Jerusalem and its environs. It is quite possible, therefore, that
'the abomination of desolation standing in the holy place'
refers to the Roman armies encircling Jerusalem.

The Hebrew *shiqquts,* translated 'abomination', refers in the
Old Testament to idols or to customs derived from idolatory.
Regarding this it has often been noted that the Roman soldiers
carried standards or ensigns consisting of images of the
emperor, eagles and various symbols drawn from paganism.
These objects received special reverence from the army and
were an 'abomination' to the Jews. Their objection to them
was so strong that regiments stationed in Jerusalem normally
left them behind at Caesarea. However, they were of course
carried by the armies that laid siege to Jerusalem in 70 A.D.
Moreover, Josephus records that when the city fell, the Romans
'brought their ensigns to the temple, and set them over
against its eastern gate; and there did they offer sacrifices to
them'.

Now we mentioned in our introductory chapter that there
are superficial similarities between the events of Antiochus's
reign and the events described in 9:26, 27. We suggested that
part of the explanation is that although these verses refer
primarily to the events of 70 A.D., there is some sort of
secondary reference to the 'tribulations' which precede the
first and second comings of Christ. The reason for our suggestion is this. When Jesus spoke about Daniel's prophecy and
the events of 70 A.D., He used a term, 'the abomination of
desolation', which is closely connected with Antiochus
Epiphanes; and at the same time he seemed to be looking
forward to the time of His second advent. Thus Antiochus's
persecution, the Jewish War of 67—70A.D. and the tribulation
preceding the second advent seem to be connected with each
other in some way — and we suggest the following link-up.

Antiochus desecrated the temple in 167 B.C., and this
desecration was repeated in 67—70 A.D. The persecution and
blasphemy which preceded the first advent typifies that

which will precede the second advent. Antiochus's persecution
and the Jewish War of 67–70 A.D. both lasted about three
and a half years, and both typify (in the book of Revelation)
the suffering of God's people during the present age, particularly during the period preceding the second event. In Daniel
9:26b, 27b (together with 12:7) these different events seem
to be superimposed on each other, or telescoped together, in a
way that is typical of Biblical prophecy — as explained in our
introduction. This will become clearer as we proceed,
especially when we come to consider the book of Revelation
in our final chapter.

The critical view

Now the critics, of course, believe that Daniel 9:24–27 refers
to the time of Antiochus Epiphanes. And as we have said, the
events described do resemble certain events in the reign of
Antiochus. But it is only a superficial resemblance — there
are important discrepancies. The critics put these down to
ignorance or over-optimism on the part of the author, and
they refuse to notice that they (the discrepancies) disappear
when the prophecy is applied to the time of Christ. These
'errors' are not errors at all. The prophecy appears to be
erroneous *only when applied to the time of Antiochus.* When
it is applied to the time of Christ, it fits perfectly.

In what ways, therefore, did the events of Antiochus's
reign appear to fulfil the predictions? The 'anointed one' who
was 'cut off', it is said, was the murdered high priest, Onias
III. The 'prince who is to come' was Antiochus Epiphanes,
whose armies partially destroyed Jerusalem and massacred
many of its inhabitants. He made a 'covenant' with the
Hellenising Jews and for 'half a week' (three and a half
years) he abolished the 'sacrifice and offering'. His crowning
'abomination' was the erection of a heathen altar on the great
altar of burnt sacrifice.

And what are the discrepancies? Firstly, there is no way in
which seventy weeks of years can be squeezed into the period
of time between the rebuilding of Jerusalem and Antiochus
Epiphanes. The events of 170–164 B.C. occurred far too early.
Secondly, most of the predictions of verse 24 were not fulfilled around the time of Antiochus. By no stretch of the

imagination can it be said that the Maccabees brought in ever-lasting righteousness or sealed up both vision and prophet. Nor can it be said (in any adequate sense) that they put an end to sins and atoned for iniquity. Thirdly, verse 26 indicates that the city and temple of Jerusalem were to be destroyed, where-as Antiochus destroyed only part of the city and he did not destroy the temple at all. Fourthly, in verse 27 a distinction seems to be made between the one who 'makes a strong coven-ant' and the one who 'makes desolate'.

The critics deal with the first of these discrepancies by dismissing the seventy weeks as 'an error of calculation'. As for the unfulfilled predictions in verse 24, these are merely aspects of a noble, but rather over-optimistic, hope. The prediction that the temple would be destroyed is more diffi-cult to explain away, however, and is therefore quietly ignored! (A second century author would have seen with his own eyes that Antiochus did not destroy the temple.)

Of course, if we believe the prophecies were faked and are full of errors, a few discrepancies here and there do not worry us. But if, in the process, we shut our eyes to a perfectly good fulfilment which has no discrepancies, are we not being rather unwise? Especially when Jesus Christ repeatedly en-dorsed the reliability of the Scriptures, and repeatedly emphasised that they had prophesied all about Him.

We stated in our introductory chapter that there are certain predictions about Christ which appear to refer also to the time of Antiochus — and this is one of them. We emphasised however, that Antiochus fulfilled these predictions *imper-fectly,* whereas Christ fulfilled them *perfectly.* We said that a possible (but highly unlikely) explanation is that a second century author *thought* he was writing about his own time only, but guided by the Holy Spirit, he was actually pointing to Christ.

If the book is a work of the sixth century, on the other hand, it may be that God introduced these ambiguities deliberately — partly to allow for a secondary fulfilment (as explained in the preceding section), and partly for much the same reason that Christ taught in parables. This amazing pre-diction of the date of Christ's coming has, in a sense, been disguised. But it is there for those who are willing to believe what the New Testament plainly teaches — namely, that His coming was foretold in great detail in the Old Testament.

Summary

To summarise, there can be no doubt, in the present writer's mind, that Daniel 9:24—27 looks forward to the time of Christ and that it is one of the most remarkable pieces of predictive prophecy in the Old Testament.

It was *perfectly fulfilled in every detail* by the coming of Christ and the destruction of Jerusalem in 70 A.D. The time of Antiochus, on the other hand, indisputably *failed to provide accurate and complete fulfilment.* Furthermore, Christ Himself indicated very clearly that verses 26 and 27 refer to the destruction of Jerusalem in 70 A.D. Less specifically, but equally clearly, the New Testament indicates that verse 24 was fully fulfilled by Christ, and Christ alone.

Note that when Christ gave His discourse on the Mount of Olives (Matthew 24), He referred to Daniel's 'abomination of desolation' *and* to his vision of the 'one like a son of man'. Also, when He referred to the 'stone' which broke the image, He was clearly thinking of God's judgment which was soon to fall upon the Jews (Luke 20:9—18). Thus there is a close connection between the visions of chapters 2 and 7 and the prediction of chapter 9 — with regard to Christ's work of salvation *and* His work of judgment. 'The coming of the Son of man' spells salvation to those who receive HIm, but judgment to those who reject Him. The destruction of Jerusalem in 70 A.D. was an early manifestation of 'the coming of the Son of man' in judgment. It was a clear and unmistakable warning that God *will* punish those who reject His Son.

Daniel prayed, '. . . cause thy face to shine upon thy *sanctuary,* which is desolate . . . behold our desolations, and the *city* which is called by thy name' (9:17, 18). God's answer was that Jerusalem would indeed be rebuilt — and that the Messiah would accomplish His work of salvation — but that *'the city and the sanctuary'* (v. 26) would be destroyed yet again.

CHAPTER SEVEN

The Image and Beasts Explained

The last three chapters of Daniel (10, 11 and 12) are a record of a single revelation given during the reign of Cyrus. In the introductory verses of chapter 10, we are told that a great spiritual battle was fought before the heavenly messenger was able to come to Daniel. It is made clear that this last revelation is of tremendous importance and significance.

In view of the vast importance attached to the vision, it comes as rather a surprise to many readers to discover the actual nature of its contents. Most of the revelation consists of a very detailed description of the history of part of the Greek empire. It is as remarkable for its apparent unimportance and irrelevance as for its immense detail. The explanation, however, is very simple.

The angel who brings the revelation says these words: 'I . . . came to make you understand what is to befall your people in the latter days. For the vision is for days yet to come' (10: 14). Comparison between these words and those of 2:28 and 8:17, 19, 26 makes it clear that the new revelation is closely connected with the earlier visions. In contrast to those visions, however, we are told that Daniel 'understood the word and had understanding of the vision' (10:1). The reason is not very difficult to see — the relevation is given in the form of a straightforward historical narrative which clearly and openly explains how the earlier visions were to be fulfilled. When Jesus preached in parables, it was His custom to give the parable and then explain it afterwards. The same order occurs in the book of Daniel. We have the symbols in the earlier visions, and they are explained in the final vision.

In chapter 11 the angel describes the course of history from the time of Cyrus (in whose reign the prophecy was given) right up to the time of the Roman empire, shortly before the birth of Christ. Practically every detail of the third and fourth kingdoms finds an explanation here in the description of Persia and Greece. After a very lengthy description of Greek history from the time of Alexander to Antiochus Epiphanes, we are treated to a description of the empire's complete destruction. This is followed, in chapter 12, by details about the arrival of the heavenly kingdom. The last event mentioned is the destruction and scattering of the Jewish nation. The vision therefore brings together the two earlier strands of prophecy and weaves them into a single thread. One strand runs through chapters 2, 7 and 8, and the other through chapter 9. They are intimately joined in this final vision of chapters 10 to 12.

This latter vision contains a historical account of quite extraordinary detail. It is so detailed, in fact, that it reads like a history book. The accuracy and detail of *this prophecy in particular* is so great that critical scholars refuse to accept that it was written before the events took place. As described already, they assign it, together with the rest of Daniel's prophecies, to the time of Antiochus's persecution. We shall see, however, that the historical section actually goes well beyond the time of Antiochus up to the year 27 B.C., long after the very latest possible date of composition.

The man clothed in linen

We are told that the thing was revealed to Daniel in the third year of Cyrus, king of Persia. He was by the river Tigris, having spent a period of three weeks in prayer and fasting, when he lifted his eyes and saw 'a man clothed in linen, whose loins were girded with gold of Uphaz. His body was like beryl, his face like the appearance of lightning, his eyes like flaming torches, his arms and legs like the gleam of burnished bronze, and the sound of his words like the noise of a multitude'. What a contrast to the lifeless metals and brute beasts (representing earthly powers) of the earlier visions! When Daniel saw this mighty heavenly being 'no strength was left in him'. He was completely overcome by the great vision.

After Daniel's strength had been restored somewhat, the

man explained that he had been sent in response to Daniel's prayer; but for the last three weeks he had been resisted and held back by 'the prince of the kingdom of Persia' — that is, the great spiritual power behind that nation. However, Michael, 'one of the chief princes', had come to his aid, so enabling him to reach Daniel and 'make him understand what was to befall his people in the latter days'. He said that he would return to fight with the prince of Persia and then the prince of Greece would come. He added that the only person helping him was 'Michael your prince'.

Some interpreters believe this heavenly being to be Christ, as his description is rather similar to that of Christ in Revelation 1. However, for the following reasons it is likely that this person is not Christ, but some high angelic authority:

1. The man speaking to Daniel does not claim in any way to be divine.

2. Daniel does not address him as a divine person.

3. The record does not indicate that he is divine, whereas in other theophanies of the Old Testament, the divinity of the Person is indicated very clearly.

4. Comparison with chapters 8 and 9 shows that Daniel's informant may well be the angel Gabriel. It is hardly surprising that Gabriel can be so awe-inspiring, seeing that he stands in the very presence of God (Luke 1:19).

5. In Revelation 15:6 we read of seven angels clothed in linen and girded with gold, and in Revelation 10:1, 5, 6 we read of a 'mighty angel' whose words and actions are closely akin to those of the man who is speaking to Daniel (12:7).

6. Daniel's informant makes repeated mention of Michael, who is 'one of the chief princes', 'your (Daniel's) prince', 'the great prince who has charge of (R.V., stands for) your people' (10:13, 21; 12:1). Michael appears to have greater claim to Daniel's allegiance than the informant and He *helps and strengthens the informant*. Regarding Daniel 11:1 (see below), we can take it that the informant helped *Darius the Mede*. There is no need to understand that it was Michael he helped.

Darius the Mede

> 'As for me (the man in linen), in the first year of Darius the Mede, I stood up to confirm and strengthen him.' (Daniel 11:1)

We have already learned that God stirred up the Medes against Babylon. Here we read that a mighty angelic power was assisting Darius the Mede in the first year of his reign, when he took over from the Babylonian kings.

The future of Persia

> 'And now I will show you the truth. Behold, three more kings shall arise in Persia; and a fourth shall be far richer than all of them; and when he has become strong through his riches, he shall stir up all against the kingdom of Greece . . .' (Daniel 11:2)

The prophecy is given during the reign of 'Cyrus king of Persia' (10:1). Daniel is told, 'three more kings shall arise in Persia', making four kings of Persia in all. The description of the fourth king is that of Xerxes, whose riches were proverbial. In 480 B.C. he launched an immense and ostentatious invasion of Greece, but he was soundly defeated at Salamis, Plataea and Mycale. The decline of Persia can be dated from this time. Her power had cracked. Her period of greatness had covered the reigns of her first four kings — Cyrus, Cambyses, Darius and Xerxes. It was they who had created her vast and fabulously rich empire. We have seen already how this verse enables us to identify the four-headed leopard of chapter 7.

The rulers which followed these first four kings are considered to be so unimportant, relatively, that they are not even mentioned. The narrative considers Persia to be politically dead or dying after the reign of Xerxes, because it now goes straight on to describe Alexander, who was stirred up against Persia partly by the memory of Xerxes' invasion.

The rise and fall of Greece

> 'Then a mighty king shall arise, who shall rule with great dominion and do according to his will. And when he has arisen, his kingdom shall be broken and divided toward the

four winds of heaven, but not to his posterity, nor accord-
ing to the dominion with which he ruled; for his kingdom
shall be plucked up and go to others besides these.' (Daniel
11:3, 4)

Here is described the irresistible might of Alexander. Following his death in 323 B.C., his empire was broken up and
reduced in size. The remains were eventually divided into four
main kingdoms (later reduced to three) which were ruled not
by Alexander's descendants, but by four of his generals —
Cassander, Lysimachus, Seleucus and Ptolemy. The reader
should note that in quick succession the narrator mentions
four great kings of the Persian empire and *four* kingdoms of
the Greek empire. This is powerful evidence that the four-
headed leopard represents Persia and does *not* represent
Greece, which was later symbolised by a four-horned he-goat.
The four Persian kings are associated with the *power* of
Persia (like the four heads of the leopard), whereas the four
Greek kingdoms are associated with the empire's decline (like
the four horns of the he-goat).

The narrative now concentrates on the Ptolemies of Egypt
and the Seleucids of Syria, as it was they who most directly
affected Israel. The former are called the kings of the south
and the latter the kings of the north.

'Then the king of the south shall be strong, but one of his
princes shall be stronger than he and his dominion shall be
a great dominion.' (Daniel 11:5)

After Alexander's death, one of his most powerful generals,
Ptolemy Soter, had himself appointed as satrap of Egypt. He
eventually made himself king in 304 B.C. One of Alexander's
lesser generals, Seleucus, took control of the far eastern
satrapies and made himself king in 312 B.C., having been under
Ptolemy's protection for a time. After the battle of Ipsus in
301 B.C., Ptolemy, Seleucus, Cassander and Lysimachus
emerged as the four most powerful rulers, but Seleucus became
ruler of by far the largest of the Greek kingdoms (incorporat-
ing Syria, Babylonia, Media etc.) and was consequently called
Nicator, 'Conqueror'.

'After some years they shall make an alliance, and the
daughter of the king of the south shall come to the king

of the north to make peace; but she shall not retain the strength of her arm, and he and his offspring shall not endure; but she shall be given up, and her attendants, her child, and he who got possession of her.' (Daniel 11:6)

In order to end his war with Antiochus Theos, who was the son of Antiochus Soter and grandson of Seleucus Nicator, Ptolemy Philadelphus gave his daughter Berenice to Antiochus. The latter thereupon divorced his former wife, Laodice, and disinherited her son. After Ptolemy died, however, Antiochus took back Laodice, who then poisoned him, caused Berenice and her son to be put to death and raised her own son, Seleucus Callinicus, to the throne.

'In those times a branch from her roots shall arise in his place; he shall come against the army and enter the fortress of the king of the north, and he shall deal with them and shall prevail.' (Daniel 11:7)

Ptolemy Euergetes, brother of Berenice, succeeded Philadelphus and avenged his sister's death by overrunning Syria and slaying Laodice.

'He shall also carry off to Egypt their gods with their molten images and with their precious vessels of silver and of gold; and for some years he shall refrain from attacking the king of the north. Then the latter shall come into the realm of the king of the south but shall return into his own land.' (Daniel 11:8, 9)

Ptolemy, on hearing of trouble back in Egypt, returned with much silver and many precious vessels and images, including Egyptian idols which Cambyses had carried from Egypt into Persia. The Egyptians were so gratified that they named him Euergetes, 'Benefactor'.

'His sons shall wage war and assemble a multitude of great forces, which shall come on and overflow and pass through, and again shall carry the war as far as his fortress.' (Daniel 11:10)

'His sons' were Seleucus Ceraunus and Antiochus the Great, sons of the king of the north, Seleucus Callinicus. Antiochus succeeded his elder brother on the throne and successfully warred with Ptolemy Philopater, Euergetes' son, until he had recovered all the parts of Syria subjugated by Euergetes.

'Then the king of the south, moved with anger, shall come out and fight with the king of the north; and he shall raise a great multitude, but it shall be given into his hand. And when the multitude is taken, his heart shall be exalted, and he shall cast down tens of thousands, but he shall not prevail.' (Daniel 11:11, 12)

Ptolemy Philopater, angered by his losses, struck back and in 217 B.C. defeated a large Syrian army at Raphia, near Gaza. He did not follow up his victory over Antiochus, but made peace with him and gave himself up to licentious living.

'For the king of the north shall again raise a multitude, greater than the former; and after some years he shall come on with a great army and abundant supplies. In those times many shall rise against the king of the south; and the men of violence among your own people shall lift themselves up in order to fulfil the vision; but they shall fail. Then the king of the north shall come and throw up siegeworks, and take a well-fortified city. And the forces of the south shall not stand, or even his picked troops, for there shall be no strength to stand. But he who comes against him shall do according to his own will, and none shall stand before him; and he shall stand in the glorious land, and all of it shall be in his power.' (Daniel 11:13–16)

Nineteen years after his defeat at Raphia, Antiochus returned with a great army and defeated Ptolemy Epiphanes, the young son of Ptolemy Philopater, at Panion. Antiochus was helped by Philip of Macedon and rebels in Egypt itself. Certain Jews also helped him besiege the Egyptian garrison in Jerusalem. If they hoped that this would cause their country to gain its independence they were disappointed, since Judaea was now brought under the sway of the Seleucids. It had hitherto belonged to the Ptolemies and had been much devastated by the continual fighting.

'He shall set his face to come with the strength of his whole kingdom, and he shall bring terms of peace and perform them. He shall give him the daughter of women to destroy

*the kingdom; but it shall not stand or be to his advantage.'
(Daniel 11:17)*

Antiochus turned to wile instead of force in his attempt to
bring all the possessions of the Ptolemies under his sway. He
gave Ptolemy Epiphanes his daughter Cleopatra in marriage,
but she favoured her husband rather than her father, so
defeating his schemes.

*'Afterward he shall turn his face to the coastlands, and
shall take many of them; but a commander shall put an end
to his insolence; indeed he shall turn his insolence back
upon him. Then he shall turn his face back toward the
fortresses of his own land; but he shall stumble and fall,
and shall not be found.' (Daniel 11:18, 19)*

Antiochus warred with Rome and took many of the Aegean
islands, but was defeated by Lucius Scipio Asiaticus at
Magnesia in 189 B.C. and ceded to Rome all Asia Minor
north and west of the Taurus mountains. Antiochus had to
return to his own land and find the money to pay the
tribute imposed by Rome. He attempted to plunder the temple
of Jupiter at Elymais and was killed by the infuriated inhabitants.

*'Then shall arise in his place one who shall send an exactor
of tribute through the glory of the kingdom; but within a
few days he shall be broken, neither in anger nor in
battle.' (Daniel 11:20)*

Seleucus Philopater, son of Antiochus the Great, succeeded
his father on the throne. He exacted much money from his
subjects (to pay the aforementioned tribute) and sent his
minister Heliodorus to plunder the temple in Jerusalem. After
a relatively short reign of twelve years (his father reigned for
thirty-six years) he was poisoned by Heliodorus, who hoped
to gain the crown thereby.

Antiochus Epiphanes

*'In his place shall arise a contemptible person to whom
royal majesty has not been given; he shall come in without
warning and obtain the kingdom by flatteries. Armies shall
be utterly swept away before him and broken, and the*

prince of the covenant also. And from the time that an alliance is made with him he shall act deceitfully; and he shall become strong with a small people.' (Daniel 11:21–23)

Antiochus Epiphanes was the younger brother of Seleucus Philopater and had been an hostage in Rome. He was on the way back to Syria when Seleucus died. Demetrius, the elder son of Seleucus, had taken his place as hostage in Rome. Employing his considerable capacity for cunning and flattery, Antiochus Epiphanes borrowed an army from the king of Pergamos and overthrew Heliodorus. He then arranged an agreement or 'covenant' whereby he was to reign jointly with the younger son of Seleucus, also named Antiochus. This joint reign or 'alliance' lasted about five years until the child was murdered. In this manner did Antiochus Epiphanes acquire the kingdom. He was 'contemptible' in that he indulged in mad escapades beneath the dignity of a king — so much so that he was nicknamed Epimanes, 'the madman'. They had not given him 'royal majesty' because he was not the rightful heir to the throne. However, everyone in his way (including the child Antiochus, 'the prince of the covenant') was 'swept away before him'. The rightful heir to the throne, Demetrius, was left sitting in Rome.

Up to this point, the chapter has been accounting for the ten horns and little horn of Daniel's fourth beast. Seleucus Philopater was the seventh Seleucid king and in his rise to power Antiochus Epiphanes, the little horn, had to displace a further three individuals — Demetrius, Heliodorus and the child Antiochus.

'Without warning he shall come into the richest parts of the province; and he shall do what neither his fathers nor his fathers' fathers have done, scattering among them plunder, spoil, and goods. He shall devise plans against strongholds, but only for a time.' (Daniel 11:24)

The narrative continues to describe Antiochus's methods. He looted and enriched himself in a way that his ancestors had never done. Polybius, the Greek historian, tells us that he 'despoiled most sanctuaries'. He bestowed lavish gifts upon his followers in order to gain support. He was constantly scheming to increase his power.

'And he shall stir up his power and his courage against the king of the south with a great army; and the king of the south shall wage war with an exceedingly great and mighty army; but he shall not stand, for plots shall be devised against him. Even those who eat his rich food shall be his undoing; his army shall be swept away, and many shall fall down slain. And as for the two kings, their minds shall be bent on mischief; they shall speak lies at the same table, but to no avail; for the end is yet to be at the time appointed.' (Daniel 11:25—27)

This describes the first of Antiochus's expeditions against Egypt. He entered Egypt with a great army of footmen, cavalry, chariots and elephants. Ptolemy Philometer was defeated owing to the treachery and incompetence of his officers and ministers. Antiochus advanced unchecked until he reached Alexandria, which he was unable to take. He captured Philometer and placed him as king at Memphis, pretending he wanted to help him against Ptolemy Physcon, whom the Egyptians had made king, as Philometer was in Antiochus's hands.

'And he shall return to his land with great substance, but his heart shall be set against the holy covenant. And he shall work his will, and return to his own land.' (Daniel 11:28)

Antiochus returned from Egypt in 169 B.C. with much loot. In his absence it had been rumoured that he had died in the fighting. Acting upon this, a former highpriest, Jason, and his followers had stormed Jerusalem and ousted Menelaus, the highpriest installed by Antiochus. On his return, therefore, Antiochus attacked Jerusalem, slaughtered many of its inhabitants, plundered and desecrated the temple and reinstated Menelaus as highpriest.

'At the time appointed he shall return and come into the south; but it shall not be this time as it was before. For ships of Kittim shall come against him, and he shall be afraid and withdraw, and shall turn back and be enraged and take action against the holy covenant. He shall turn back and give heed to those who forsake the holy covenant. Forces from him shall appear and profane the temple and

fortress, and shall take away the continual burnt offering. And they shall set up the abomination that makes desolate.'
(Daniel 11:29—31)

Ptolemy suspected Antiochus's designs and hired mercenaries from Greece. In 168 B.C., therefore, Antiochus advanced towards Egypt with a large army and fleet. But this second expedition had an ending very different from that of the first, because Ptolemy had also asked the Romans for help. The Roman ambassador, Popilius Laenas, waited until he had the news of Rome's victory in a war with Macedon and then immediately sailed to Ptolemy's aid. This victory over Macedon (during the reign of Antiochus Epiphanes) marked the beginning of the Greek empire's collapse and break-up. Popilius met Antiochus at Eleusis, four miles from Alexandria, and presented him with the Senate's decree that he was to keep out of Egypt. Antiochus replied that he would consider the matter, but Popilius haughtily drew a line round him with a rod and informed him that he was to give a reply before he left the circle. Antiochus had to submit and withdrew north again, seething with anger and humiliation. He gave vent to his wrath by turning on the Jews. He sent an army which fell upon Jerusalem, slaughtering many, taking others as slaves and looting and partially destroying the city. In 167 B.C. orders were given that the temple ritual must be suspended, that the sacred scriptures must be destroyed, that the Sabbath and other festival days be no longer observed, that the strict food laws be abolished and that the rite of circumcision be discontinued. The culminating attack on Jewish worship came in December, when an altar and probably also an image ('the abomination that makes desolate') were erected in the temple court and dedicated to the worship of Olympian Zeus. (The historian of I Maccabees plainly records that an 'abomination of desolation' was set up on the altar.) Similar altars were set up throughout Judaea and the Jews were ordered to sacrifice at them. Disobedience was rewarded with severe penalties and the result of all this was a savage and barbaric persecution. The Hellenizing Jews who forsook Judaism and embraced the Greek culture were favoured and honoured.

> *'He shall seduce with flattery those who violate the covenant; but the people who know their God shall stand firm and take action. And those among the people who are wise shall make many understand, though they shall fall by sword and flame, by captivity and plunder, for some days. When they fall, they shall receive a little help. And many shall join themselves to them with flattery; and some of those who are wise shall fall, to refine and to cleanse them and to make them white, until the time of the end, for it is yet for the time appointed.' (Daniel 11:32–35)*

As mentioned already, Antiochus flattered and favoured the Jews who forsook Judaism for the Greek culture. The faithful Jews, on the other hand, wrote a glorious chapter in the history of Israel. They were subjected to the most appalling persecution, but they remained true throughout it all. Many had to endure torture and death. It was not long, however, before the priest Mattathias and his sons raised the standard of revolt. In the hills they gathered a guerilla band around them and, led by Judas Maccabeus, they repeatedly defeated the armies of Antiochus. This is the probable meaning of 'they shall receive a little help'. Many joined the faithful 'with flattery' when they saw that the war was going favourably for Judas.

Note the words, 'until the time of the end'. We were told that the vision of the ram and the he-goat concerned 'the time of the end'. The he-goat symbolised Greece, and its little horn symbolised Antiochus Epiphanes. We are now told that the saints would suffer under Antiochus 'until the time of the end'. Again, it is apparent that Antiochus and the Greek empire were destroyed *at the time of the end.*

Up to this point, verse 35, there is general agreement concerning the interpretation of the narrative. The next section, verses 36 to 39, has caused some disagreement. Although it can be applied to Antiochus, some conservative interpreters assert that he fulfilled it only partially. However, we shall see that in fact he did fulfil it completely. The section describes his general policy and, in particular, it shows why he made such a determined attempt to eradicate Judaism. We are told in verse 36 that he would prosper 'till the indignation is accomplished'. Compare this with the statement that the doings of Antiochus, as related in the vision of the he-goat, took place 'at the latter end of the indignation' (8:19).

> *'And the king shall do according to his will; he shall exalt himself and magnify himself above every god, and shall speak astonishing things against the God of gods. He shall prosper till the indignation is accomplished; for what is determined shall be done.' (Daniel 11:36)*

Antiochus did exactly what he liked. He called himself *Theos Epiphanes,* 'God Manifest', regarding himself as the incarnate manifestation of Olympian Zeus, whom he set up as the greatest of gods. He blasphemed the God of Israel, but he prospered only for as long as God had ordained.

> *'He shall give no heed to the gods of his fathers, or to the one beloved by women; he shall not give heed to any other god, for he shall magnify himself above all. He shall honour the god of fortresses instead of these; a god whom his fathers did not know he shall honour with gold and silver, with precious stones and costly gifts.' (Daniel 11:37, 38)*

Antiochus did not honour Apollo, the traditional protector of the Seleucid dynasty, but instead he raised up Olympian Zeus as the chief god of his kingdom and he himself claimed to be his incarnation — thus his real god was himself. The head of Zeus replaced the head of Apollo on Seleucid coins. 'The one beloved by women' may have been Tammuz, a Syrian deity (see Ezekiel 8:14 — 'there sat women weeping for Tammuz'). All this was part of a plan to strengthen and unite his kingdom by giving it one Hellenic culture and religion. Antiochus was in fact seeking to mingle the iron of Greece with the clay of the conquered peoples, as pictured by the image's feet of iron and clay. The iron sought to mingle with the clay, and so strengthen it. This strengthening of the kingdom against external and internal dangers through cultural and religious unity may help to explain what is meant by 'the god of fortresses'. The term may also refer to the fact that Antiochus enforced the worship of his god with the help of soldiers and fortresses, particularly the hated citadel at Jerusalem, the Akra. The following verse shows that this god was also used to *overcome* fortresses — it was used to break down resistance.

> *'He shall deal with the strongest fortresses by the help of a foreign god; those who acknowledge him he shall magnify with honour. He shall make them rulers over many and shall divide the land for a price.' (Daniel 11:39)*

One of the strongest fortresses Antiochus had to overcome was that of the Jewish religion. In verse 31 the centre of Jewish worship, the temple, is called a 'fortress', the same word, *maoz,* being used (see R.V.). The orthodox Jews strongly opposed Antiochus's efforts to impose on them a pagan Greek culture and religion. The Jewish 'clay' refused to mingle with the Greek 'iron'. Antiochus therefore decided that Judaism must be stamped out completely and the cult of Zeus must be imposed forcibly. He tried to overcome the fortress of Judaism by enforcing the worship of Olympian Zeus — a strange god indeed to the Jews. Those who 'acknowledged' him (the Hellenizing Jews), he 'magnified with honour' and 'made them rulers over many'. Amongst these Jews was Menelaus, the false high priest, who had obtained his office with the aid of a large bribe ('a price').

The destruction of the Greek empire

We now come to the final and most controversial section of chapter 11. Superficially it appears to continue the description of Antiochus — yet it bears no relation whatever to his actual historical career. Critical scholars point to this as major evidence for a second century B.C. date of authorship during the reign of Antiochus. They inform us that this last section of the chapter is the unknown author's hopeful, but inaccurate prediction of the future career and eventual destruction of Antiochus — the first part of the chapter being, of course, an accurate description of *past* history.

Conservative scholars usually overcome the difficulty by assuming that Daniel suddenly jumps thousands of years and starts describing the 'Antichrist'. Reading chapter 11, however, one is given little or no reason to suspect that this extraordinary gap exists between verses 39 and 40 (or 35 and 36, verses 36 to 39 often being included as part of the description of the Antichrist). The final section has every appearance of being a direct continuation of the preceding verses and we shall see that in fact it accurately describes the destruction of the Greek empire and the arrival of Rome. The section is a detailed historical account *of the same type* as the preceding verses. It is most unlikely that the narrative should suddenly take a jump of over two thousand years and calmly continue describing history in the same sort of detail as before. The existence of the interpretation outlined below should make such an unnatural solution to the problem quite unnecessary. Moreover, to project the section into the future would again *totally ignore Christ's first advent.* We have already seen how completely this is at variance with New Testament teaching.

The section begins at verse 40 with the words, *'At the time of the end'.* As we have seen, the goal of Daniel's prophecy is the advent of the Messiah; therefore these words probably carry us nearer this event. Let it be noted, however, that we are still in the region of the Greek era, because we are specifically told that the vision of the ram and the he-goat in chapter 8 concerns *'the time of the end'* and that the he-goat represents Greece (8:17, 21). Daniel has made it clear that the sign of Christ's imminent arrival will be the destruction of the Greek empire. He has described the career of Antiochus, 'the beginning of the end', so he now goes straight on to describe the final destruction of the Greek empire (the destruction of the body of the fourth beast).

The Romans began their conquest of the Greek empire during the reign of Antiochus by defeating Macedon in 168 B.C. It was fully incorporated into the empire a few years later, when it was made a Roman province in 148 B.C. Rome was now the paramount power in the East, but she did not proceed to annex any land there until 65 B.C., when Syria was absorbed into the Roman empire, Jerusalem being taken by Pompey in 63 B.C. Egypt was more or less at the mercy of Rome, but was not made an imperial province until 27 B.C. Verses 40 to 43 are an excellent description of the arrival of Rome in the East.

> *'At the time of the end the king of the south shall attack him; but the king of the north shall rush upon him like a whirlwind, with chariots and horsemen, and with many ships; and he shall come into countries and shall overflow and pass through. He shall come into the glorious land. And*

> *tens of thousands shall fall, but these shall be delivered out*
> *of his hand: Edom and Moab and the main part of the*
> *Ammonites. He shall stretch out his hand against the*
> *countries, and the land of Egypt shall not escape. He shall*
> *become ruler of the treasures of gold and of silver, and all*
> *the precious things of Egypt; and the Libyans and the*
> *Ethiopians shall follow in his train.' (Daniel 11:40—43)*

In verse 40 we have an ambiguity. We are told that a king
of the north shall rush upon 'him'. This 'him' could be the
king of Egypt, but another possibility is that it is the same
'him' as the one who comes earlier in the verse — that is, the
king of Syria. The correct translation throughout the chapter
should really be '*a* king of the south' and '*a* king of the
north'. It is possible, therefore, that verse 40 should be understood as follows. 'At the time of the end a king of the south
(Egypt) shall attack him (Syria); but a king of the north
(Rome) shall rush upon him (Syria) like a whirlwind etc.'

In the first part of verse 40 the central figure is the king of
Syria, as in the preceding passage; but the words 'at the time
of the end' have transported us on a number of years to the
closing years of the Greek empire. The king of Syria is no
longer Antiochus Epiphanes — he is now Antiochus Asiaticus,
the last of the Seleucid monarchs. This interpretation may
appear at first sight rather unconvincing, but if the reader
just reads on, he will find it fully justified.

The rest of the passage graphically describes the progress
of Rome. Pompey's legate, Scaurus, arrived in 65 B.C. and
annexed Syria. Pompey himself arrived on the scene later and
started out on a campaign against the Nabataeans in 63 B.C.
The Nabataeans were a powerful Arab tribe which had occupied the old kingdoms of Edom to the south, Moab to the
south-east and Ammon to the north-east of the Dead Sea.
However, Pompey did not complete the campaign. He post-
poned it (indefinitely) in order that he might settle the
quarrels of rival Jewish leaders. Thus the Nabataeans retained
their independence, and Edom, Moab and most of Ammon
remained outside the Roman empire (a small section of
Ammon lay within the Roman territories of Peraea and
Decapolis). Pompey proceeded to Jerusalem and captured the
city without much difficulty; and so the Jews were again under

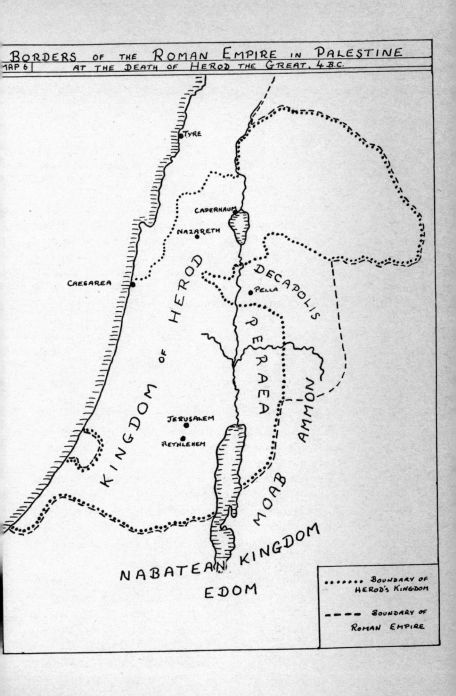

BORDERS OF THE ROMAN EMPIRE IN PALESTINE

MAP 6 AT THE DEATH OF HEROD THE GREAT, 4 B.C.

Tyre

Capernaum

Nazareth

Caesarea

DECAPOLIS

Pella

KINGDOM OF HEROD

PERAEA

AMMON

Jerusalem

Bethlehem

MOAB

NABATEAN KINGDOM

EDOM

••••••• BOUNDARY OF HEROD'S KINGDOM

— — — BOUNDARY OF ROMAN EMPIRE

foreign domination after only a few short years of independence. As mentioned already, Egypt lay within the power of Rome, but was not made an imperial province until 27 B.C. Libya and Ethiopia, both of which bordered Egypt, were indeed 'at the steps' (R.V.) of Rome. This amazing chapter closes with verses 44 and 45, which read,

> *'But tidings from the east and the north shall alarm him, and he shall go forth with great fury to exterminate and utterly destroy many. And he shall pitch his palatial tents between the sea and the glorious holy mountain; yet he shall come to his end, with none to help him.' (Daniel 11: 44, 45)*

These last two verses refer to the ever-present threat to the Roman empire of the Parthians in the North-East. In 54 B.C. Crassus undertook a campaign against the Parthians (he, Pompey and Julius Caesar were the members of the First Triumvirate); but before the campaign *he took over the province of Syria and pillaged it very thoroughly, also plundering the treasures of the temple in Jerusalem.* Doubtless he pitched his tents between the Mediterranean and Mount Zion at some stage. His campaign was unsuccessful, however, and he was killed by the Parthians — thus did he 'come to his end'. After Pompey and Julius Caesar had died, Augustus finally became emperor. It was during his reign that Jesus Christ was born.

We can see, therefore, that verses 40 to 45 are a perfect description of the destruction of the Greek empire and the arrival of the Romans. This interpretation is so accurate and so completely in context, that it must surely be the correct one.

. Now the chief objection to our interpretation of verses 40 to 45 is that there is no clear indication that the identity of the 'king of the North' has changed. In the previous verses the 'king of the North' has always been a Greek king of Syria, and one would naturally assume that the same goes for these verses. This objection may be answered as follows.

The words 'at the time of the end' *are* an indication — even if not a particularly obvious one — that the 'king of the North' has changed his identity. The words are extremely significant, and form a definite break or turning point in the narrative. Daniel has already shown that at the time of the end

Greece will be destroyed, following the death of Antiochus Epiphanes, and that this will precede the coming of the kingdom of Heaven. Since this section follows a description of Antiochus Epiphanes, precedes a description of the kingdom of Heaven and is introduced by the words 'at the time of the end', we should expect it to concern the destruction of Greece. If we take it that it is describing this, it is reasonable to assume that the destroying 'king of the North' here is some new non-Greek character. In view of the fact that the description does not apply to any Greek king of Syria, but does apply perfectly to the nation which destroyed the Greek empire, one might say it is more than reasonable.

Note also the way in which the words 'and the land of Egypt shall not escape' are tacked onto the end of verses 40 to 42.

> 'At the time of the end a king of the south shall attack him; but a king of the north shall rush upon him like a whirlwind . . . he shall come into countries and shall overflow and pass though. He shall come into the glorious land . . . He shall stretch out his hand against the countries, and the land of Egypt shall not escape.'

These words do not suggest a king of the north whose *prime target* (v. 40) is the king of Egypt. The impression we get is of some *outside power* attacking the whole area, beginning with Syria. Egypt is only one of the victims, and a late one at that.

The structure of verse 40 does allow this interpretation. Indeed, in the present writer's opinion this way of understanding verse 40 is the most natural one. Note again that the correct translation throughout the chapter should be *a* king of the north, not *the* king of the north. The phrase simply indicates a king to the north of Israel — it does not have to be the Syrian king.

Another difficulty with our interpretation is the fact that Antiochus's death — a very important event — is not described. This is a fairly weighty objection, and we shall deal with it in some detail later in the chapter. In the meantime, we can note that there is some hint of this event in verse 36. In that verse it is implied that Antiochus will prosper *only for as long as God has ordained.*

Another difficulty, in some people's minds, may be the gap in time between verses 39 and 40. In fact this gap can be explained very easily. In the vision of the four beasts, the death of the little horn was followed by the destruction of the body of the fourth beast. The narrative of chapter 11 corresponds to this by describing the career of Antiochus and then going straight on to describe the destruction of the Greek empire. The intervening period of time is irrelevant and therefore not described. (Note that this is also true of Persian history after the first four great kings. Daniel 11:2 describes the first four kings of Persia — corresponding to the four heads of the leopard — and then, completely ignoring the later kings of Persia, goes straight on in verse 3 to describe Alexander.)

The last section describing the Romans' failure against the Parthians may seem slightly irrelevant to the main idea of the prophecy, which is the destruction of the Greek empire in preparation for the coming of Christ. But one function this small section does perform is that of showing that Daniel's fourth kingdom (as described in 2:33, 40 and 7:7, 23) is *not* badly defeated even before she had finished subjugating the Greek empire and while she was still in her prime. This does not agree with the picture we have of the iron-hard, all-conquering fourth kingdom. Secondly, these verses draw attention to the fact that the Romans did not by any means tread down 'the whole earth'. The Parthians ruled a very large part of the former Babylonian, Median, Persian and Greek empires, and we have already noted that in the context of the book of Daniel 'the whole earth' must surely include the area covered by those empires.

Another function performed by 11:44, 45 is that of showing how 7:12 was fulfilled. In 7:11 we were told that the fourth beast was killed and 'its body destroyed and given over to be burned with fire'. This is explained by the account of Rome's annexation of Syria in 11:40—43. In 7:12 we were told, 'As for the rest of the beasts, their dominion was taken away, but their lives were prolonged for a season and a time'. This is explained by the account of Rome's failure against Parthia in 11:44, 45. *Because of this failure, Babylonia, Media and Persia all remained outside the Roman empire.* Their dominion was taken away, but they were independent of Rome.

We said in chapter 3 that Daniel 11:40—45 describes in a very remarkable way how 7:11, 12 was fulfilled — and this has now been explained. It seems safe to say that our interpretation of 11:40—45 is more than adequately justified. In the introductory chapter of this book, it was stated that the course of history is described in accurate detail *right up to the time of Christ,* and that this fact more or less completely demolishes one of the critical scholars' major arguments for a second century B.C. date of authorship. As we have seen, the events taking place *after* the reign of Antiochus are described in just as accurate detail as the events before and during his reign.

The four kingdoms

Let us pause for a moment and try to see how this chapter links up with the previous ones, and how it shows us that the 'four kingdoms' are indeed Babylon, Media, Persia and Greece.

To begin with, in his introductory remarks the man in linen says, 'I will return to fight against the prince of Persia; and when I am through with him, lo, the prince of Greece will come' (10:20). Note that Persia is not coupled with Media here and that there is no mention of Rome following Greece.

When we come to the actual revelation, we find that it is preceded by a brief mention of the *Median* king who took over from the Babylonian kings. The second verse speaks of four great *Persian* kings who very definitely correspond to the four powerful heads of the third beast. The next forty-one verses deal at extraordinary length with *Greece.* Note the Babylon-Media-Persia-Greece sequence with the emphasis on Greece.

The irresistible might of Alexander corresponds to the fourth kingdom's initial phase of immense power, represented by the legs of iron. The empire after Alexander's death corresponds to the kingdom's second phase of division and weakness, represented by the feet of iron and clay. The ten horns and little horn of the fourth beast are clearly identified by the detailed description of the kings of Syria and Antiochus Epiphanes. The destruction of the Syrian Greek empire corresponds to the destruction of the image and also the body of the fourth beast. The annexation of Egypt can be included as part of the destruction of the image. It was completed in 27 B.C. and brings us up to about twenty years before the birth of Christ. Rome's failure against Parthia shows us how the first three beasts escaped destruction with the fourth beast. At the same time it shows us that Rome was not the fourth kingdom.

That the fourth kingdom was Greek is confirmed by the extraordinary detail with which the Greek empire and Antiochus are described and by their close similarity to the fourth kingdom and the little horn. In addition to this we are given details about the Roman empire which more or less completely exclude any possibility of its being the fourth kingdom.

The critics answered

To critical scholars, Daniel 11:40–45 is an extremely important passage. Not only do these scholars believe it to be one of the few attempts at genuine prediction in the book, but they also believe that it enables us to establish the date of authorship with considerable accuracy. If 11:2–39 is an accurate record of *past* history, and 11:40–45 is an inaccurate prediction of *future* history, it fixes the date of authorship at shortly before 164 B.C.

In the light of our discovery that verses 40 to 45 describe the destruction of the Greek empire by Rome, how should we view the critical position? Firstly, we can say quite categorically that these verses contain *accurate* predictions of events leading up to the time of Christ. These predictions are just as accurate and just as detailed as those in the preceding verses — and they correspond exactly to certain details in the visions of chapters 2 and 7. It is clear therefore that the most important argument for a second century date of authorship is completely wrong and should be discarded.

We have seen that the gap in time between verses 29 and 40 is easily explained, but how do we explain the fact that Antiochus's death is not described? And how do we explain the fact that verses 40 to 45 do give a superficial impression of continuing to describe Antiochus? It could be argued that a second century author *thought* he was describing the last days of Antiochus, but guided by the Holy Spirit, he was actually describing the destruction of the Greek empire by Rome. But this is most unlikely — there is absolutely no need to postulate a second century date of authorship.

The most likely explanation is that this is another case of 'prophetic foreshortening'. Historically, the death of Antiochus Epiphanes and the final destruction of the Syrian Greek empire were two events separated by a period of about a hundred years. But in 11:40—45 the two events are telescoped together and represented as one event. The death of Antiochus Epiphanes is identified with the destruction of the Syrian Greek empire. The reason for this is that both these two happenings were parts of a single event — namely, the destruction of 'antichrist', the fourth beast.

Another explanation which follows on from this, and is another aspect of the 'prophetic foreshortening', is the traditional conservative view that these verses look forward to the last great 'Antichrist'. We have noted already that the prophecies of Daniel may have more than one fulfilment. Antiochus and the Syrian Greek empire may well typify some future antichrist. Daniel 11:40—45 undoubtedly does describe the destruction of the Greek empire by Rome; but it may well be that it also looks forward to the last great 'Antichrist'. The destruction of the Greek antichrist — Antiochus and the Syrian Greek empire — typifies the eventual destruction of the last 'Antichrist'. This is apparent from Revelation 13:1—18 and 19:19, 20 (as we shall see in our final chapter) and also from II Thessalonians 2:1—12.

> 'Now concerning the coming of our Lord Jesus Christ . . . that day will not come, unless the rebellion comes first, and the man of lawlessness is revealed, the son of perdition, who opposes and exalts himself against every so-called god or object of worship, so that he takes his seat in the temple of God, proclaiming himself to be God . . . the Lord Jesus will slay him with the breath of his mouth and destroy him by his appearing and his coming . . .' (II Thessalonians 2:1—12)

We suggest that God introduced this ambiguity in Daniel 11:40—45 *deliberately* (as in the case of 9:24—27) — partly for the above reasons, and partly for much the same reason that Jesus taught in parables. This particular passage is of enormous significance, since it brings us right up to the time of Christ. It has, in a sense, been disguised; but it is there for those who are willing to believe what the New Testament plainly teaches — namely, that Christ's coming was foretold in great detail in the Old Testament.

CHAPTER EIGHT

The Great Prince

We are now coming to the final part of the revelation. If indeed chapter 11 does end with the destruction of the Greek empire, we can anticipate, in the light of previous chapters, that the Messiah will now come into the picture. This is what we read:

'At that time shall arise Michael, the great prince who has charge of your people. And there shall be a time of trouble, such as never has been since there was a nation till that time; but at that time your people shall be delivered, every one whose name shall be found written in the book. And many of those who sleep in the dust of the earth shall awake, some to everlasting life, and some to shame and everlasting contempt. And those who are wise shall shine like the brightness of the firmament; and those who turn many to righteousness, like the stars for ever and ever.' (Daniel 12:1—3)

This abundantly confirms our expectations. The prophets indicated that the coming of the Messiah would be associated with *a time of great trouble* (Jeremiah 30:5—9). The Jews certainly believed that the Messiah would *deliver them* (Jeremiah 23:5, 6), but most were blind to the fact that only those who are *written in God's book* would be saved (Isaiah 4:2—4). *The resurrection of the dead* had been foretold (Isaiah 26:19), also the abolition of death and coming of joy *for ever* (Isaiah 25:8; 35:10).

Having confirmed that these verses probably do refer to the coming of the Messiah, let us now see how they were fulfilled.

Michael

Firstly, we must identify Michael. His name means 'Who is

like God?'. He is 'first of the chief princes' (10:13, Young's Literal Translation), 'your (Daniel's) prince' (10:21), 'the great prince which standeth for the children of thy people' (12:1, R.V.), 'the archangel (chief angel)' (Jude 9). In the book of Revelation Michael is depicted as head over all the angels of God.

It is generally taken that Michael is the guardian angel of the Jews. However, Daniel 12:1 indicates that he is more than this — *he is the prince of those who are written in God's book, the Lamb's book of life.* In Revelation 12:7 we find that it is he who fights and vanquishes Satan. This is no ordinary angel — not even the highest ranking of the angels created by God. This, surely, is Jesus Christ Himself. It is Christ who bruised the serpent's head, bound the strong man, destroyed the works of the devil, brought to nought him that had the power of death and triumphed over principalities and powers. We are told that Satan and his angels warred against Michael and His angels (Revelation 12:7). We are later told that Satan's earthly puppet (the beast) and his armies war against Christ and the heavenly army (Revelation 19:19). It is likely, surely, that if Christ is needed to crush Satan's earthly puppet, Christ is also needed to crush Satan himself. Christ, we are told, will descend from heaven with a shout, *with the voice of the archangel,* and the dead shall rise. Christ said, 'All that are in the tombs shall hear his (Christ's) voice, and shall come forth' (I Thessalonians 4:16; John 5:28, 29).

Michael may well be the mysterious, divine 'Angel of the Lord' — also called the angel of his presence and the messenger (angel) of the covenant. This is indicated by Jude 9 and Zechariah 3:1–4. In Jude we find Michael contending with the devil[1] and saying, 'The Lord rebuke you' and in Zechariah we find the Angel of the Lord contending with Satan and saying, 'The Lord rebuke you'.

The 'Angel of the Lord' appears quite frequently in the Old Testament, and it is clear that on a number of occasions (including Zechariah 3) the Being is none other than God

---

1.   In the light of II Peter 2:10, 11, the fact that Michael 'did not presume to pronounce a reviling judgment upon him' suggests that He is 'greater in might and power' than Satan.

Himself.[2] In one particular case the Angel is shown to be not
only the Lord Himself, but also the 'guardian angel' of Israel.

> 'Behold I send an angel before you, to guard you on the
> way and to bring you to the place which I have prepared.
> Give heed to him and hearken to his voice, do not rebel
> against him, for he will not pardon your transgression; for
> my name is in him. But if you hearken attentively to his
> voice and do all that I say, then I will be an enemy to your
> enemies and an adversary to your adversaries.' (Exodus 23:
> 20—22)

This angel may well, like Michael, be described as 'the
guardian angel of Israel'. The passage quoted suggests that the
angel is actually divine, and the following verses confirm this:

> 'And the Lord went before them by day in a pillar of cloud
> to lead them along the way, and by night in a pillar of fire
> to give them light, that they might travel by day and by
> night.' (Exodus 13:21).

> 'Then the angel of God who went before the host of Israel
> moved and went behind them; and the pillar of cloud moved
> from before them and stood behind them . . .' (Exodus 14:
> 19)

Here the Person in the pillar of cloud and fire is described
as 'the Lord' and also as 'the angel of God'. We suggest that
the guardian angel of Israel is none other than Jesus Christ
Himself.

It is generally acknowledged that the 'Prince of the host'
(Daniel 8:11) is God Himself and that 'the host' refers to the
faithful Jews. Michael is described to Daniel as 'the great
prince which standeth for the children of thy people' (12:1,
R.V.). It looks as if the 'Prince of the host' and Michael are
one and the same person. The natural conclusion is that
Michael is God Himself. The 'Prince of the host' was also
called 'Prince of princes' (8:25) — Christ is called 'King of
kings, and Lord of lords' (Revelation 19:16).

There are some interesting words in Zechariah 12, a chapter

---

2.   E.g., Genesis 48:16; Exodus 3:2—6; cf. Joshua 5:13—15; Isaiah
     63:8, 9; Malachi 3:1, 2.

which probably predicts the Jewish military victories and religious revival in the days of Antiochus Epiphanes, as well as applying spiritually to the true Israel and heavenly Jerusalem.

'On that day the Lord will put a shield about the inhabitants of Jerusalem so that the feeblest among them on that day shall be like David, and the house of David shall be like God, like the angel of the Lord, at their head.' (Zechariah 12:8)

The 'angel of the Lord at their head' may refer to the divine Angel that led the children of Israel in the wilderness. This chapter in Zechariah appears to deal with the times of both Antiochus Epiphanes and the Christian church, so this verse forms yet further evidence that the divine Angel of the Lord, the Prince of the host, Michael and Jesus Christ are one and the same Person.

At the very outset of the conquest of the promised land, Christ appeared to Joshua and revealed Himself to be both the Prince of the host and the Angel of the Lord (Joshua 5:13–15). Joshua saw a Man standing over against him with His sword drawn in His hand. Joshua went up to Him and asked Him whether He was friend or foe. The reply was, 'Nay; but as captain of the host of the Lord am I now come' (R.V.). 'Captain' translates the word *sar,* which is translated 'prince' in Daniel 8:11. Thus this Man was none other than the 'prince of the host' of Daniel 8. Joshua fell on his face to the earth and worshipped Him, and said, 'What does my lord bid his servant?'. The Prince of the Lord's host answered, 'Put off your shoes from your feet; for the place where you stand is holy'. And Joshua did so. The Man had also revealed Himself to be the divine Angel of the Lord who had been leading Israel, because when the Angel of the Lord called to Moses out of the burning bush, He said, 'Put off your shoes from your feet, for the place on which you are standing is holy ground — I am the God of your father, the God of Abraham, the God of Isaac, and the God of Jacob'. And Moses hid his face; for he was afraid to look at God (Exodus 3:5, 6). The Angel went on to tell Moses that His name was I AM. Over a thousand years later, Jesus said, 'Truly, truly, I say to you, before Abraham was, *I am*'; and the Jews tried to stone Him for blasphemy (John 8:58, 59).

The belief that Michael is Christ is by no means new; but owing to the heretical ideas usually associated with it, it has been condemned by the orthodox in the past — although this attitude is changing now. In fact the belief is perfectly scriptural. Michael is described as 'the archangel', which means the chief angel — and note that in the Bible, Michael is the *only* archangel. An angel (messenger) is one who is 'sent', and Christ repeatedly claimed that He was 'sent' by God the Father. 'I proceeded and came forth from God; I came not of my own accord, but he sent me (John 8:42).

Having said all this, we can see that there are very strong grounds for believing that Michael is Jesus Christ, the Son of God, the Messiah.

The kingdom of heaven

> '*At that time shall arise Michael, the great prince who has charge of your people. And there shall be a time of trouble, such as never has been since there was a nation till that time . . .' (Daniel 12:1a)*

This little section begins with the words, 'At that time'. The following section (verses 1b—3) begins with the same words — 'but *at that time* your people shall be delivered, every one whose name shall be found written in the book . . .'.

To the present writer it appears that verse 1a outlines in a nutshell the work of the Messiah and its sequel, as described already in Daniel 9. In that prophecy we were told that Christ's redeeming work was to be followed by war, desolation and the destruction of Jerusalem. In this section likewise, it is stated that Christ was to stand up in redeeming power, but there was to be a time of great trouble. Having made this summarising statement, the prophecy then concentrates (verses 1b—3) on the Messiah's work of redemption, opening again with the words 'at that time'.

We have already shown that Michael represents Christ. We must now establish the meaning of 'at that time', and the identity of the 'time of trouble'. The words 'at that time' come at the beginning of Daniel 12. Clearly 'that time' must refer to the latter part of chapter 11, which was all about Antiochus and the destruction of the Greek empire. Michael is called here the 'prince' of Israel, and it is stated that He 'arose' at the time of the destruction of the Greek empire. This links up with

1. The fact that in chapter 8 we are told Antiochus rose up against the 'Prince' of Israel, but was broken by no human hand, and
2. The fact that the visions of the image and four beasts indicate the Messiah began setting up His kingdom by destroying Antiochus and the Greek empire.

Now for the 'time of trouble'. This is identified for us by Jesus Christ Himself. When He warned His disciples of the coming Jewish War and siege of Jerusalem, He said,

'Pray that your flight may not be in winter or on a sabbath. For then there will be great tribulation, such as has not been from the beginning of the world until now, no, and never will be.' (Matthew 24:20, 21)

These words suggest that the great 'time of trouble' is the Jewish War, which culminated in the siege and destruction of Jerusalem in 70 A.D. This is the same picture as the one we find in chapter 9. The redemptive work of the Messiah will be associated with a terrible war which will culminate in the desolation of the city and temple of Jerusalem. The greatest time of trouble the world has ever seen came upon the people who crucified the Son of God. 'His blood be on us, and on our children', they cried. It has been, with vengeance.

Note that Daniel's words suggest a time of *national* trouble. The Jewish War was national calamity on an unprecedented scale. The Jewish nation was wiped off the map for nearly two thousand years, and vast numbers of Jews were slaughtered or sold into slavery. Over a million perished in the siege of Jerusalem alone.

In parenthesis, we should also note that Jesus's words differ slightly from Daniel's. He did not mention the word 'nation', and He added that there would never be such great trouble again. Jesus was undoubtedly speaking of the Jewish War (cf. Luke 21:20—24), but it is possible He was also looking beyond it up to the final tribulation which is to precede His second advent.

We have dealt with the introductory section, so let us now proceed to the following section.

'... *but at that time your people shall be delivered, every one whose name shall be found written in the book. And many of those who sleep in the dust of the earth shall awake, some to everlasting life, and some to shame and everlasting contempt. And those who are wise shall shine like the brightness of the firmament; and those who turn many to righteousness, like the stars for ever and ever.' (Daniel 12:1b–3)*

These verses describe what Michael or Christ achieved when He 'arose' in conquering and redeeming power. In Revelation 12 Christ's work of deliverance is symbolised by the battle between Michael and the dragon. The dragon is finally cast out of Heaven and a voice is heard saying, 'Now the salvation and the power and the kingdom of our God and the authority of his Christ have come'. This shows that the defeat of the dragon symbolises Christ's work of redemption and the setting up of the Messianic kingdom. Jesus said, 'Now is the judgment of this world, now shall the ruler of this world be cast out' (John 12:31).

The section we are considering begins, 'But at that time your people shall be delivered, every one whose name shall be found written in the book'. The deliverance referred to is the deliverance from sin, Satan and death made possible by Christ's victorious death and resurrection.

'Blessed be the Lord God of Israel, for he has visited and redeemed his people, and has raised up a horn of salvation for us in the house of his servant David, as he spoke by the mouth of his holy prophets from of old ...' (Luke 1:68–70).

'Your people' would at first sight appear to mean Daniel's fellow-Jews. However, the qualification 'every one whose name shall be found written in the book' clearly limits 'your people' to those who are true children of God, those who are written in the Lamb's book of life (Revelation 21:27). It also brings in all the Gentiles who are children of Abraham

by faith (Romans 4:16, 17; Galatians 3:7, 14, 28, 29). Thus
we can see that Michael's work of deliverance is to be identified with Christ's work of atonement and victory over death
and hell.

The section we are considering continues,

> *'And many of those who sleep in the dust of the earth shall
> awake, some to everlasting life, and some to shame and ever-
> lasting contempt. And those who are wise shall shine like
> the brightness of the firmament; and those who turn many
> to righteousness, like the stars for ever and ever.' (Daniel
> 12:2, 3)*

Here Daniel goes on to describe further the consequences of
Christ's victory over death and hell when He died and rose
again some two thousand years ago. Nowhere else in the Old
Testament is the glorious certainty of resurrection and eternal
life stated so clearly. Christ was probably thinking of Daniel's
prophecy when He forecast His return in the following words:

> '. . . the hour is coming when all who are in the tombs will
> hear his voice and come forth, those who have done good,
> to the resurrection of life, and those who have done evil,
> to the resurrection of judgment.' (John 5:28, 29)

> 'The Son of man will send his angels, and they will gather
> out of his kingdom all causes of sin and all evildoers, and
> throw them into the furnace of fire; there men will weep
> and gnash their teeth. Then the righteous will shine like
> the sun in the kingdom of their Father . . .' (Matthew 13:
> 41–43)

On the face of it, Daniel seems to be predicting the general
resurrection at the time of the second advent – and in a
secondary sense he *is* doing this. But as with the rest of
Daniel's prophecies, the *primary* reference is to something
which took place at the time of the first advent. Note that
whereas Daniel only said 'many' shall 'awake', Jesus said 'all'
shall 'come forth' when He returns at the end of the world.
Daniel is primarily speaking of a limited 'awaking' that
occurred when Michael 'arose' some two thousand years ago.
When we turn to the New Testament we find that in fact there
was an 'awaking' of the dead at the time of the first advent.

'Truly, truly, I say to you, the hour is coming, and now is, when the dead will hear the voice of the Son of God, and those who hear will live.' (John 5:25)

'And he said to him, "Truly, I say to you, today you will be with me in Paradise." ' (Luke 23:43)

'. . . and the earth shook, and the rocks were split; the tombs also were opened, and many bodies of the saints who had fallen asleep were raised, and coming out of the tombs after his resurrection they went into the holy city and appeared to many.' (Matthew 27:51—53)

'Christ . . . being put to death in the flesh but made alive in the spirit; in which he went and preached to the spirits in prison . . .' (I Peter 3:18, 19)

'. . . but they will give account to him who is ready to judge the living and the dead. For this is why the gospel was preached even to the dead, that though judged in the flesh like men, they might live in the spirit like God.' (I Peter 4:5, 6)

After His death, Christ apparently proclaimed the news of His completed work of salvation to those who had 'fallen asleep'. John 5:25 refers partly, at least, to the spiritually dead; and the meanings of I Peter 3:18, 19 and 4:5, 6 are much disputed. However, the verses quoted above do seem collectively to indicate that Jesus proclaimed the gospel to the dead after He was crucified. In the Old Testament, Sheol, the abode of the dead, is represented as a place of complete darkness, forgetfulness and oblivion.[3] Dying, therefore, was aptly pictured as a 'falling asleep'. The 'awaking' of those who slept is therefore a good picture of what happened when Christ went into Sheol and proclaimed the gospel. Those who were righteous awoke to be taken with Him to Paradise, and those who were unrighteous awoke only to find they were under shame and contempt. The word 'many' is used rather than 'all', perhaps, because it speaks only of those who died before Christ, rather than the total number of all those who will have died before the end of the world.

3.   Job 10:21, 22; Psalms 6:5; 30:9; 88:10—12; 115:17; Ecclesiastes 9:10; Isaiah 38:18.

In John 5:28, 29 (quoted a few paragraphs back) Jesus took Daniel's words and, having altered them slightly, applied them directly to the second advent. But in so doing, He was perhaps developing the idea in Daniel and giving the words a degree of meaning they did not originally possess — He dealt in a rather similar way with the 'stone' and perhaps with the 'time of trouble' and the 'Son of man coming with the clouds of heaven'. Christ's defeat of death two thousand years ago was the bud of which the resurrection at the last day will be the full flower. The awaking described by Daniel was the general resurrection in embryo. In fact Jesus was probably referring to the awaking which took place at the time of the first advent *as well as* the general resurrection at the time of the second advent. He was thinking of the awaking described by Daniel, but He was also looking beyond it to the general resurrection at the last day.

Daniel's words about the resurrection are so strongly reminiscent of those describing the saints who were persecuted by Antiochus (8:10; 11:33) that they were probably meant to be a special encouragement to those who suffered for their faith, including those who actually were persecuted by Antiochus.

'Some were tortured, refusing to accept release, that they might rise again to a better life.' (Hebrews 11:33b)

The book of Revelation also gives special encouragement to those who suffer for the cause of Christ. They are assured that if they 'overcome' and are faithful to the end, they will sit with Christ on His throne and will live and reign with Him a thousand years. This is called the 'first resurrection'. The events which Revelation depicts as taking place after the 'thousand years' are, according to the rest of the New Testament, to take place at the end of the age in which we are living *now*. The present writer believes that this means we are living in the 'thousand years' of Revelation *now*, and that the 'first resurrection' occurs as soon as Christ's redeemed depart this life — we go to reign with Him. But it is a spiritual resurrection, not a physical one. 'The second resurrection' will be the resurrection of both the just and the unjust, when Christ returns after the 'thousand years' at the end of the world. For the just it will be a bodily resurrection in preparation for the new heaven and the new earth and for the unjust it will be a resurrection to judgment and the 'second death'. This whole question of the 'thousand years' will be dealt with at slightly greater length in our final chapter.

Could it be that Daniel's 'awaking' of the sleepers has something to do with the 'first resurrection'? When the righteous sleepers awoke and were taken with Christ to Paradise, were they taking part in the first resurrection? It seems that there is an earlier 'resurrection' of the righteous which first occurred at the time of Christ's first advent; but there will be another resurrection of the *whole* world (the 'second resurrection') at the time of His second advent. Every time a believer dies, and goes to be with Christ, he or she takes part in the first resurrection — and this has been happening ever since Christ died and rose again.

The angel concludes the prophecy with the following words:

'*... But you, Daniel, shut up the words, and seal the book, until the time of the end. Many shall run to and fro, and knowledge shall increase.*' (Daniel 12:4)

This probably means that towards the time of the end many people will 'run to and fro' through Daniel's prophecies. They will eagerly examine the prophecies and begin to understand them in the light of the events taking place around them.

How long till the end of these wonders?

One could quite easily take the next section (12:5—7) as referring to the time of Antiochus Epiphanes — because in a superficial way it does appear to do this. But as with 9:24—27, there is far more to this passage than meets the eye at first glance. We noted that 9:24—27 appears *superficially* to refer to Antiochus; but when we examine the passage closely, we find that the real reference is to the coming of Christ and the destruction of Jerusalem in 70 A.D. We shall see that almost exactly the same thing can be said about 12:1—7. We have dealt already with the first four verses, so we proceed now to 12:5—7.

'*Then I Daniel looked, and behold, two others stood, one on this bank of the stream and one on that bank of the stream. And I said to the man clothed in linen, who was*

*above the waters of the stream, "How long shall it be till
the end of these wonders?" The man clothed in linen, who
was above the waters of the stream, raised his right hand
and his left hand toward heaven; and I heard him swear by
him who lives for ever that it would be for a time, two
times, and half a time; and that when the shattering of the
power of the holy people comes to an end all these things
would be accomplished.' (Daniel 12:5—7)*

To the critical scholar it is obvious, as we have said, that
this passage, together with 11:40—12:4, refers to the time of
Antiochus Epiphanes. The 'time, two times, and half a time'
refers to the three and a half years of Antiochus's persecution.
And the 'shattering of the power of the holy people' refers to
the persecution itself. The second century author believed that
after a period of three and a half years, 'all these things would
be accomplished'. That is, the death of Antiochus, the deliverance of faithful Jews and also, presumably, the resurrection of
the dead (11:40—12:3).

Needless to say, we reject this interpretation. There can be
no doubt, as far as we are concerned, that these prophecies
look forward to the coming of Jesus Christ. As far as we know,
the resurrection of the dead (12:2, 3) certainly did not take
place around the time of Antiochus Epiphanes! And as we
have seen, 11:40—45 does not describe the last days of
Antiochus. It describes the final destruction of the Greek
empire. It should also be noted that Antiochus's persecution
lasted three and a *division* (*pelag*) times in 7:25 — not three
and a *half* (*chatsi*) times, as in 12:7. And last, but not least,
Antiochus did *not* shatter the power of the Jews.

Assuming that these prophecies look forward to the time
of Christ, therefore, how are we to interpret this passage?
Daniel is told that all the things he has been shown in this
vision will be accomplished 'when the shattering of the power
of the holy people comes to an end'. We learn from 8:24 that
'the holy people' means Israel. 'Shatter' translates the word
naphats, which means to beat or dash in pieces and spread
out. Chapter 9 indicates that the Messiah's work of establishing the New Covenant was to be sealed by the siege and destruction of Jerusalem and the desolation of the Jewish people.
And we have seen that the same event is referred to in 12:1.

We are told that Michael shall arise and 'there shall be a time of trouble, such as never has been since there was a nation till that time'. We have seen that Jesus indicated that this 'time of trouble' was the siege and destruction of Jerusalem and the desolation of the Jewish people in 70 A.D. We are now told (12:7), '. . . when the shattering of the power of the holy people comes to an end all these things will be accomplished'. In the present writer's opinion, there can be little doubt that the angel is speaking here about the events of 70 A.D. — when the power of the Jews was truly shattered. (Note, however, that as with Daniel 9:26b, 27b, there is a secondary link-up with the 'tribulations' which precede the first and second comings of Christ.)

This last prophecy, like that of chapter 9, deals with the nation of Israel, to a large extent, because at the beginning Daniel's informant said, 'I came to make you understand what is to befall your people in the latter days' (10:14). The nation's history as God's covenant people came to an end in 33 A.D. God set His outward and visible seal on this event by destroying the nation and scattering the people in 70 A.D. This is where the prophecy comes to an end. The kingdom of Christ had been born; but as Jesus predicted (Matthew 21:41, 43), the Jews had to be severely punished for rejecting their Messiah, and the kingdom was taken away from them and given to 'a nation producing the fruits of it' (that is, to the true, spiritual Israel).

We read that the breaking in pieces of the power of the holy people will be completed after 'a time, two times, and half a time', that is, 1260 days (360 x 3½). 'Half' on this occasion does mean 'half', because it translates *chatsi,* meaning 'half' or 'middle'. Vespasian set out from Antioch in the spring of 67 A.D. and began the bloodbath which was completed by his son Titus, approximately *three and a half years* later in September, 70 A.D., when he destroyed the temple and city of Jerusalem. We shall see later that Revelation 12 indicates the Jewish War lasted three and a half 'times' and it is specifically stated that this period was one of 1260 days.

Final hints

Daniel is still mystified, however, and asks, 'What shall be the

issue of these things?'. Daniel's informant does not answer
this question, but says,

> '*Go your way, Daniel, for the words are shut up and sealed
> until the time of the end. Many shall purify themselves, and
> make themselves white, and be refined; but the wicked shall
> do wickedly; and none of the wicked shall understand; but
> those who are wise shall understand. And from the time
> that the continual burnt offering is taken away, and the
> abomination that makes desolate is set up, there shall be a
> thousand two hundred and ninety days. Blessed is he who
> waits and comes to the thousand three hundred and thirty-
> five days. But go your way till the end; and you shall rest,
> and shall stand in your allotted place at the end of the
> days.*' (Daniel 12:9—13)

The man clothed in linen tells Daniel that many shall purify
themselves, but the wicked shall do wickedly. Comparison with
Daniel 11:32—35 makes it apparent that the messenger is
referring again to the time of Antiochus's persecution. This is
confirmed by the words which follow regarding the taking
away of the continual burnt offering and the setting up of
the abomination that makes desolate (cf. 11:31). We are told
that the wise shall understand (Daniel's prophecies), but the
wicked shall not. It is in fact generally agreed that the Jews
who were persecuted by Antiochus did read Daniel's prophecies, and were greatly strengthened and encouraged thereby.

We are told that from the time that the continual burnt
offering shall be taken away (this being followed by the
setting up of the abomination that makes desolate) there shall
be 1290 days. This is very strong evidence that the little horn
of the fourth beast is Antiochus, because 1290 days is a period
of three 'times' plus a fraction of a time (7:25). If we count
back 1290 days from December, 164 B.C. (the time at which
the temple sacrifices were restored) we come to June, 167 B.C.
As we have seen already, it was at about this very time that
Antiochus caused the 'continual burnt offering' to be 'taken
away'. Note that in 7:25 the 1290 days are described as
being three times and a *division* of a time (*pelag*). In 12:7,
however, the Jewish War is said to last exactly three times and
half a time (*chatsi*). Revelation 12 indicates that this was a

period of 1260 days, confirming the importance and amazing accuracy of Daniel's use of *pelag* and *chatsi*.

The question of whether Antiochus's persecution and the Jewish War really did last for exactly 1290 days and 1260 days, respectively, is probably both unanswerable and unimportant. The important point is that both events did last for approximately *three and a half years* — a period of great symbolical significance (as we shall see in our final chapter). As for the thirty-day difference between 1290 and 1260, this may well symbolise something which Jesus said about the Jewish War — 'And if those days had not been shortened, no human being would be saved; but for the sake of the elect those days will be shortened' (Matthew 24:22).

The messenger goes on to say, 'Blessed is he who waits and comes to the 1335 days'. This is 45 days more than the 1290 days, and it appears to bring us on to February, 163 B.C. We ask ourselves what event of significance took place at about this time — and there is an answer. *The death of Antiochus Epiphanes.* The exact date of his death is not known, but it is reckoned that it was in the spring of 163 B.C. When the news of the Jews' successes reached Antiochus, he was on campaign in Media. His fury knew no bounds and he vowed a terrible revenge on the Jews; but he died soon afterwards at Tabae, in Persia. He was struck down by a mysterious and horrible illness in which the Jews saw the hand of God.

It will now be asked, why was Antiochus's death of such great significance? Again, there is an answer. Antiochus's death was a very special sign of the imminent arrival of the Messiah. In a general way, it marked the beginning of 'the time of the end' (8:19; 11:35, 40). It is the event with which the vision of Daniel 8 closes — we are told that Antiochus 'shall even rise up against the Prince of princes; but by no human hand, he shall be broken'. It was the triumphant work of Christ — it was the sign that He had begun the process of setting up the kingdom of Heaven. It signalled the beginning of the chain of events which culminated in the arrival of the Messiah. It was the slaying of the little horn — and was the sign that the fourth beast had also been slain. It was the sign that the 'Stone' had begun to pulverise the great image of Nebuchadnezzar's dream.

We now ask, why is Daniel told, *'Blessed is he who waits*

and comes to the 1335 days'? The answer, surely, is that those who waited upon God were told to look for more than the restoration of the temple sacrifices — they were told to look for the coming of the kingdom of Heaven. There was general rejuicing when the temple sacrifices were restored, but the people of God looked beyond this event; they watched and waited for the sign that the Messiah had laid bare His arm, the sign that He had indeed begun to destroy finally the fourth beast, the sign that the kingdom of Heaven was near. Some Jews may have thought privately that the Maccabees, rather than God, were responsible for the restoration of temple worship; but God made it quite plain that He was responsible for the event of prime importance — Antiochus's death.

This helps to explain a rather puzzling sentence in 11:34 — 'they shall receive a little help'. 'They' refers to the saints and the 'little help' apparently refers to the exploits of Judas Maccabeus and his followers. The puzzling feature is the playing down of the part played by the latter. The explanation is the fact that although these freedom fighters were of immense importance in the eyes of the Jews, they were of relatively small importance in God's wider plan. God did not have to depend on them to achieve His purposes. The Maccabees destroyed neither Antiochus nor the Greek empire. The former died at God's hand through an illness, and the latter was destroyed through God's instrument, the Roman empire — as described so accurately in Daniel 11:40—45. And although the Maccabees managed to end the Greek tyranny in Israel, in fact they replaced it with one of their own. In the long run, therefore, they were quite literally no more than a 'little help'.

The book of Daniel closes with the following words:

'But go your way till the end; and you shall rest, and shall stand in your allotted place at the end of the days.' (Daniel 12:13)

We can trust that Daniel awoke to life when Christ entered Hades and that he is now reigning in glory with Him.

The last days

In our final chapter we shall show that the three and a half

years of persecution by Antiochus *symbolises the age in which
we are living now.* The age in which the church of Christ is
persecuted by the forces of evil, but out of which it will emerge
triumphant. In a sense, therefore, the angel *did* answer Daniel's
question, 'What shall be the issue of these things?'. He
replied,

> '... *And from the time that the continual burnt offering
> is taken away, and the abomination that makes desolate is
> set up, there shall be a thousand two hundred and ninety
> days. Blessed is he who waits and comes to the thousand
> three hundred and thirty-five days.'* (Daniel 12:11, 12)

There can be no doubt that this 'abomination that makes
desolate' was set up by Antiochus Epiphanes. But Jesus Christ
also applied it to the events of 70 A.D.; and Daniel 9:27
speaks of Christ causing the 'sacrifice and offering to cease'
(when He died on the cross). Moreover, the angel has just been
speaking about the Jewish War of 67–70 A.D. (12:7).

The 1290 days of Antiochus's persecution *symbolises* the
present age, which began with the first advent of Christ and
the destruction of Jerusalem in 70 A.D. The end of the 1335
days, when Antiochus was destroyed, *symbolises* the time
when the forces of evil (the Antichrist?) will be destroyed at
the end of this age, at the time of Christ's second advent.

'Blessed is he who waits and comes to the thousand three
hundred and thirty-five days.' Blessed is he who remains
faithful to Christ, even to the end. Blessed is he who is found
ready and watching for Him when He returns.

But this is not all. The number 1335 has appeared in recent
history in a very remarkable way. To the Christian church and
to the Jewish people, 1917 is a year of enormous significance.
This was the year in which the Ottoman empire was defeated
and Jerusalem was liberated. It was also the year of the
'Balfour Declaration', in which Britain, the liberating power,
declared that she viewed with favour the establishment of a
national home for the Jews in Palestine. Jesus prophesied that
following the siege of 70 A.D., Jerusalem would be trodden
down by the Gentiles *until the times of the Gentiles are fulfilled* (Luke 21:20–24). The liberation of Jerusalem and the
return of the Jews was therefore a very special fulfilment of
prophecy.

Now the interesting thing from the point of view of Daniel's prophecies is that in the Muslim calendar, 1917 A.D. was the year 1335. The appearance of this highly unusual number in connection with a highly unusual and significant event may be no more than a very remarkable coincidence. On the other hand, it may be that God is trying to tell us something here.

We have said that the number 1335 was connected with the death of Antiochus, and that this event (which resulted in Jerusalem being liberated from the hand of a tyrant) was the sign that Christ had begun the process of setting up the king- dom of Heaven — the sign that the coming of the Messiah was near. Could it be that the defeat of the Ottoman empire and the liberation of Jerusalem was a sign that the present age is coming to a close and that the second coming of Christ is near? Does the parable of the fig tree coming out in leaf refer in part to the formation of the state of Israel?

'And he told them a parable: "Look at the fig tree, and all the trees; as soon as they come out in leaf, you see for yourselves and know that the summer is already near. So also, when you see these things taking place, you know that the kingdom of God is near." ' (Luke 21:29—31).

This strange number 1335 carries a very real message. Apart from possibly telling us that Christ's return is near, God is assuring us that *He is still in control.* He is still working His purposes out in history. The defeat of His enemies and the vindication of His saints is certain. Christ really is coming again.

May we be found ready and watching for Christ when He returns, so that when we stand in our allotted places 'at the end of the days', it will be a day of rejoicing and not a day of remorse.

CHAPTER NINE

Michael, the Dragon and the Fifth Beast

We have now come to the end of the prophecies of Daniel. We have seen that the book describes in detail the course of history from the time of Daniel up to the time of Christ; and the author hopes he has demonstrated this convincingly.

The author believes that apart from clearing up one or two minor points, this book (together with the author's published articles) has made three significant contributions to our understanding of Daniel's prophecies. Firstly, it shows that the four kingdoms are *accurate,* true-to-history descriptions of Babylon, Media, Persia and Greece. Secondly, it shows that the prophecy of the 'seventy weeks' (9:24, 25) really does predict the date of Christ's first advent. Thirdly, it shows that Daniel 11:40—45 is not an erroneous prediction of how Antiochus was to meet his fate; it is an accurate prediction of how the Greek empire was to be destroyed.

The special significance of the two latter prophecies (9:24, 25 and 11:40—45) is that both predict with great accuracy events which took place *after* the time of Antiochus Epiphanes. These prophecies must be accepted as genuine predictions, even if we believe in a second century date of authorship. In both cases critical scholars have dismissed the predictions as 'erroneous', because they appear to be inaccurate *when applied to the time of Antiochus Epiphanes.* If these scholars heeded the clear teaching of the New Testament, they would see that both prophecies pointed in a most wonderful way to the coming of Jesus Christ.

The prophecies of the 'four kingdoms' (with which 11:40—45 is linked) also pointed to the coming of Christ, because they indicated that God's kingdom would begin to fill the earth *after the total destruction of the Greek empire.*

We reject completely the critical view that Daniel's prophecies contain historical errors and mistaken predictions. We also reject any interpretation which stops at Antiochus Epiphanes and fails to take into account the coming of Christ. We reject these views because they are *demonstrably wrong* and also because they are, in our opinion, incompatible with the teaching of Jesus.

The Bible does not speak of a people who searched for God and invented a religion. It speaks of *a God who revealed Himself to men.* As for the prophecies of Daniel, they show that God is in control of world history and that it is leading up to the consummation foreordained by Him. They reveal Christ in the context of world history, and through their remarkable predictions they provide further, powerful evidence that He is indeed the Messiah, the Son of God, the Saviour of the world.

The present age

In this book we have concentrated, so far, on showing that Daniel's prophecies were accurate, and that they foretold the date and historical setting of Christ's first coming. In this final chapter we shall examine their relevance to the present age; but again we shall deal with only one aspect of the subject — the historical one — and we shall do so in a rather unusual way. We shall *not* attempt to apply the prophecies to our own situation in a devotional way. This has already been done very adequately by other authors.

The present writer has already made it clear that he believes there is an element of 'foreshortening' or 'telescoping' in Daniel's prophecies. His vision of God's kingdom includes both the first and the second advents of Christ. The writer has also indicated that he believes the events of the past age *typify* certain aspects and events of the present age — and to a large extent it is this theory that we shall be dealing with in the present chapter.

Before proceeding, however, we should question whether the prophecies may have a more specific type of fulfilment in our own day. The present writer believes that in general, it is wrong to apply the prophecies to the present age in a detailed way. Nevertheless, he feels that there is one such interpretation which may be *partly* true. This interpretation holds that the four beasts of Daniel 7 represent empires which will arise shortly before the second advent. This theory is based on the fact that the words 'shall arise' (7:17) were spoken after the rise of Babylon.

We have seen that the 'four empires' of Daniel's vision found their primary fulfilment in Babylon, Media, Persia and Greece; but there is still the possibility of a secondary, less detailed fulfilment. In the preceding chapter we noted that there are indications that Christ's second coming may be near. One more indication, which we did not mention, is that Christ said, 'This gospel of the kingdom will be preached throughout the whole world, as a testimony to all nations; and then the end will come'. This prediction seems close to fulfilment *in our own day*. If the above theory is partly correct, and if Christ's return is near, one or more of the secondary 'four empires' may have appeared already.

If this is so, Daniel's first beast could be a picture of Anglo-American power, and the second beast a picture of Russian power. The British *lion* and the American *eagle* are familiar symbols (remember that the lion had eagles' wings), and so is the Russian *bear*. The British empire was the vastest (and perhaps the noblest!) that the world has seen. The way in which the first beast was made to stand like a man and was given the mind of a man could be said to describe the humaneness of the British empire in its later stages. Although it is no longer what it was, much remains in the form of the English-speaking world (including the U.S.A., an ex-colony of the British empire). The English-speaking peoples and the Russians together destroyed Hitler's Germany, just as Babylon and Media together destroyed Assyria. The material and cultural wealth of Russia is inferior to that of the English-speaking world, just as the quality of Media was inferior to that of Babylon. The balance of power between America and Russia is similar to the balance of power between Babylon and Media. Even now we can see the scales of power beginning to tip in favour of Russia, just as they tipped in favour of Media.

If (a big if) this interpretation is correct, we can anticipate that Russia will fade and be succeeded by a world-ruling third empire. If the Medo-Persian pattern is duplicated, this third empire could be formed by a vassal state (or some other communist state) overcoming and uniting with Russia, and then conquering the entire world. This empire will then be crushed by another and more terrible world-empire, ruled by the Antichrist. In some way this fourth empire will be 'different' from the preceding empires, and shortly before the return of Christ it will make an all-out attempt to destroy the Christian church.

(Note that Babylon lay to the West of Media, and Persia to the South. Also that Babylon formed an alliance with Persia in order to stave off the threat from Media. It is interesting that Britain and her allies lie to the West of Russia, and China to the South. The Chinese are related to the people of Asiatic U.S.S.R., and also they share a communist system of government. Despite this, China hates and fears the Russians, and even now she is trying to form an alliance with the West. This is partly to counter the growing power of Russia, but also she wants help in the modernisation and development of her industry — and of her armed forces. Doubtless she looks forward to the day when she will be strong enough to overwhelm the Russians, and then the rest of the world. Whatever friendly things she may say just now, her ultimate goal is world communism. With her vast, well-ordered population and long history of civilisation, she certainly has the human resources to run a world empire. And with the technology of Japan and the West to help her, it may not take her very long to achieve her ambition. Thus history is repeating itself, but on a much bigger scale than in those far-off days, two thousand five hundred years ago.)

This is all pure speculation, of course, and it may well prove to be completely wrong; but the parallels between Babylon and Media on the one hand, and the 'British Lion' and the 'Russian Bear' on the other are rather striking. History does repeat itself; so there may be some truth in this theory. In fact the present writer feels that there may be a certain amount of truth in each of the various schemes of interpretation. Each school has something of value to contribute. With regard to the rather detailed interpretation outlined above, there is no certainty about its validity and we would do well to adopt a 'wait and see' attitude. However, it *is* possible to relate Daniel's prophecies to present and future events with a good deal more certainty, but in a less specific way; and we shall now proceed to do this.

The book of Revelation

In trying to discover how Daniel's prophecies should be applied to our own day, it will be helpful to take a brief look at the New Testament apocalypse, the book of Revelation. That it will be helpful should be apparent from the way in which we have referred to it several times already in the course of our study.

The most helpful exposition of Revelation which the present writer has come across is *More than Conquerors*, by W. Hendriksen.[1] Hendriksen believes that the book of Revelation describes the whole of this present dispensation — the age which began with Christ's first advent and will end with His second advent. In a series of visions we are again and again taken through the whole age, beginning with the first advent and ending with the second advent. The visions are *parallel*. They describe the same period of history, but concentrate on different aspects. Note that this is very similar to the scheme in the book of Daniel. In a series of parallel visions, Daniel describes history up to the first coming of Christ. Revelation continues the story by describing history from the first to the second comings of Christ.

Let it be noted, however, that Daniel and Revelation have at least one big difference. Daniel carefully and in minute detail describes the actual course of history. The eleventh chapter is an obvious example of this. Revelation describes rather certain *principles* of history which apply to the whole of the present age — it does not go into the details of specific events in the way that Daniel does. And this is what we would expect, because Christ stressed that we cannot know the date of the second advent. Revelation does describe the first advent and the second advent. These events can be identified clearly. The intervening period, however, is described in general terms only.

1. Another helpful book, which came out after this chapter was first written, is *I Saw Heaven Opened*, by Michael Wilcock.

Now the book of Revelation is deeply rooted in the Old Testament. Nearly all the symbolism is from the Old Testament, and a good deal of it comes from Daniel. We shall now go through Revelation very briefly, taking particular note of those parts which are closely connected with the book of Daniel and which therefore help us to understand its relevance to the present age.

The risen Messiah

In the first chapter, John records his stupendous vision of the risen Christ. His description of Christ's appearance is similar to (though even more awe-inspiring than) that of the great angel of Daniel 10. In both cases the description is that of a mighty heavenly being. However, whereas Daniel gave no indication whatever that the angel he saw was divine, the being of Revelation 1 clearly identifies Himself as the divine Christ. 'Fear not, I am the first and the last, and the living one; I died, and behold I am alive for evermore, and I have the keys of Death and Hades.'

This vision of Christ gives us some faint idea of His majesty, power and glory.

In the second and third chapters we find the letters to the seven churches. They describe conditions which are typical of churches throughout the age.

The Messiah's coronation

In chapters 4 and 5 John describes a scene which Daniel witnessed over six hundred years earlier — the scene of Christ's coronation (Daniel 7). In Revelation Christ is symbolised by 'a Lamb standing, as though it had been slain, with seven horns and with seven eyes'. The Lamb advanced to the throne and took a book 'from the right hand of him who was seated on the throne', and the beings around the throne (four living creatures and twenty-four elders) sang,

> ' "Worthy art thou to take the scroll and to open its seals, for thou wast slain and by thy blood didst ransom men for God from every tribe and tongue and people and nation, and hast made them a kingdom and priests to our God, and they shall reign on earth." Then I looked, and I heard . . .

the voice of many angels . . . saying with a loud voice, "Worthy is the Lamb who was slain, to receive power and wealth and wisdom and might and honour and glory and blessing!" And I heard every creature in heaven and on earth . . . saying, "To him who sits upon the throne and to the Lamb be blessing and honour and glory and might for ever and ever!" ' (Revelation 5:9—13)

Now compare this passage with Daniel 7:13, 14, 27:

'I saw in the night visions, and behold, with the clouds of heaven there came one like a son of man, and he came to the Ancient of Days and was presented before him. And to him was given dominion and glory and kingdom, that all peoples, nations, and languages should serve him; his dominion is an everlasting dominion, which shall not pass away, and his kingdom one that shall not be destroyed.' (Daniel 7:13, 14)

'And the kingdom and the dominion and the greatness of the kingdoms under the whole heaven shall be given to the people of the saints of the Most High; their kingdom shall be an everlasting kingdom, and all dominions shall serve and obey them.' (Daniel 7:27)

John and Daniel are surely describing one and the same event — Christ's coronation following his victorious death and resurrection.[2] The climax of Daniel's visions is the Heavenly scene of Daniel 7. Daniel's prophecies *end* with Christ's coronation and the establishing of the Messianic kingdom. The prophecies of Revelation *begin* with this event.

Note that Revelation 5:9—13 does much to explain the relationship between the 'one like a son of man' and 'the saints of the Most High'. Some interpreters deduce from Daniel 7:27 that the one like a son of man does not symbolise Christ at all — he symbolises the saints. Revelation 5:9—13 clearly explains that *Christ* received power and glory and the kingdom, and He *gives* it to the saints whom He has redeemed with His blood.

Suffering and disasters

The book which the Lamb took was sealed with seven seals.

2.   Compare also Revelation 5:11 with Daniel 7:10.

In chapter 6 the Lamb opens the seals one by one. Each opening is followed by scenes symbolical of various forms of
suffering and persecution which recur again and again during
the age. Their purpose is to turn men to God and to purify
and strengthen the faith of the saints. The concluding verses
symbolically describe the cataclysmic destruction of the world
at the end of the age. Already we have been brought right
through to the end of the age.

Chapter 7 describes the sealing of the hundred and forty-
four thousand, representing the church. Chapter 8 begins with
the opening of the seventh seal and proceeds with the seven
'trumpets'. As each trumpet is sounded, John sees scenes
symbolising various calamities and disasters which repeatedly
afflict the earth during the age. The trumpets are trumpets of
warning. By these disasters, God is warning the world of coming judgment.

The mighty angel

The seventh trumpet was yet to sound when John saw a mighty
angel descending from Heaven. The appearance, actions and
words of this angel are very similar to those of the great angel
of Daniel 10–12. Note particularly the following words.

> *'And I heard the man clothed in linen, which was above
> the waters of the river, when he held up his right hand and
> his left hand unto heaven, and sware by him that liveth for
> ever that it shall be for a time, times, and an half; and
> when they have made an end of breaking in pieces the power
> of the holy people, all these things shall be finished. And I
> heard, but I understood not: then said I, O my Lord, what
> shall be the issue of these things? And he said, Go thy way,
> Daniel: for the words are shut up and sealed till the time
> of the end.' (Daniel 12:7–9, R.V.)*

'And the angel which I saw standing upon the sea and upon
the earth lifted up his right hand to heaven, and sware by
him that liveth for ever and ever, who created the heaven
and the things that are therein, and the earth and the
things that are therein, and the sea and the things that are
therein, that there shall be time no longer: but in the days
of the voice of the seventh angel, when he is about to

sound, then is finished the mystery of God, according to the good tidings which he declared to his servants the prophets.' (Revelation 10:5–7, R.V.)

The reader should observe that Daniel's question was not answered. He was told when 'these things' (the things he had just been told) would be finished; but he was not told what was to happen afterwards. We gather that there was still something to follow. In Revelation, however, the angel's words seem to be quite final and conclusive.

The three and a half times

At this point we have the vision of the city and the two witnesses. And we are introduced to the period of 'three and a half times', familiar to us from the book of Daniel. This period is mentioned several times in Revelation, once as 'three and a half times', twice as 'one thousand two hundred and sixty days', and twice as 'forty-two months'. We suggest (with Hendriksen) that it symbolises the whole of the present age from the time of Christ up to just before the second advent.

For the early Christians, this period of three and a half years had very special associations. In Elijah's day the church was persecuted for three and a half years, but not destroyed. Despite the persecution, God's power was made manifest, and His people were miraculously preserved (I Kings 17–19, James 5:17). In the days of Antiochus Epiphanes, the church was savagely persecuted for three and a half years, but was not destroyed (Daniel 7, 8, 11 and 12). The public life and ministry of Jesus lasted, it seems, for three and a half years (Daniel 9:27). He was opposed and persecuted, but He emerged triumphant. And in the days of the early Christian church, Israel was ravaged by the Romans for three and a half years; but the church was preserved (Daniel 9 and 12). Because of Christ's warning, the Christians fled into the wilderness and so escaped the slaughter.

It is because of these associations that this period of three and a half years is used in Revelation to describe the present age. Throughout its history the church has had to (and will have to) undergo trials and tribulations; but God has always preserved it and it has maintained its witness. Revelation teaches, however, that at the end of the age Satan will gather his forces together against the church in one last desperate onslaught. It appears that the church will be silenced for a very short period, but this will be immediately followed by Christ's second advent. The figure three and a half is half the 'perfect' number seven and symbolises, perhaps, the temporary nature of the tribulation. God is allowing it to go on for 'a little time' only (Revelation 6:11).

In Revelation 11 the three and a half-year period is mentioned twice. We are told that the nations are to tread the holy city under foot for forty-two months, but the temple of God and they that worship therein are to be kept safe. It is likely that the three and a half-year Jewish War and siege of Jerusalem is at the back of this picture of the world's siege against the church. The true church is kept safe, but everything false is trampled underfoot and defiled.

We then read of the 'two witnesses' who are to prophesy for one thousand two hundred and sixty days. Comparison with I Kings 17—19 and James 5:17 makes it clear that this picture was partly inspired by the episode of Elijah's three and a half-year contest with Ahab. Satan is unable to prevent the witness of the church during the present age. In chapter 20 this is symbolised by his binding with a chain.

The two witnesses are finally killed and lie dead for three and a half days 'in the street of the great city . . . where their Lord was crucified'. They are then raised up and ascend into Heaven. This indicates, perhaps, that the church will finally be silenced for a very short period preceding the second advent. It also indicates that this vision is based largely on the three and a half-year ministry of Jesus, His crucifixion, His 'three days and three nights' in the grave and His resurrection. Daniel 9 indicates that there were three and a half years between Christ's baptism and crucifixion. In Revelation 11 this symbolises the period between the 'baptism' of the church, when it was anointed with the Holy Spirit at Pentecost and began to witness, and the time when it will be silenced for a short period at the end of this age. Just as Jesus was apparently defeated at the close of His ministry, but emerged triumphant, so the church will be apparently defeated at the close of this age, but will emerge triumphant.

(Note that this vision was recorded in the first century A.D., and is powerful evidence that Christ's public ministry really did last three and a half years.)

Michael and the dragon

The book of Revelation is divided into two main sections, the second one opening with chapter 12. In the earlier chapters we see the church suffering trial and tribulation in the world. In the later chapters we see the deeper spiritual conflict which underlies this struggle with the world. We see that it is a struggle between Christ and Satan.

At the start of chapter 12 we are again taken back to the beginning of the age, the first advent. We see a woman wearing a crown of twelve stars. She clearly represents the church, the Israel of God. 'The church' and 'the Israel of God' are terms which cover the whole people of God, including those who lived before the time of Christ. The woman gives birth to a child, the Messiah, who is then caught up to God and His throne. These events are associated with *the flinging of a dragon (Satan) from Heaven by Michael,* after which a loud voice is heard saying, 'Now the salvation and the power and the kingdom of our God and the authority of his Christ have come'.

Let the reader cast his mind back to the first words of Daniel 12. 'At that time shall arise Michael, the great Prince who has charge of your people . . . at that time your people shall be delivered, every one whose name shall be found written in the book.' The meaning of these words is made plain to us in Revelation 12. The words refer to Christ's work of salvation at the time of the first advent. This picture of the Messiah being born of a woman and then caught up to Heaven places the work of Michael fairly and squarely at the beginning of the present age — the time of the first advent.

The dragon, knowing he has not long to live now, desperately persecutes the woman; but God enables her to flee into the wilderness, where she is nourished for one thousand two hundred and sixty days (verse 6), or three and a half 'times' (verse 14). Here again we meet our period of three and a half years. It represents the present age during which Satan seeks to destroy the church; but the church is preserved by God.

This picture of the flight into the wilderness could be inspired by the story of Elijah, and also by the escape of the Christians during the war with Rome. Elijah fled into the wilderness and was nourished by God for three and a half years. Likewise the Christians fled into the wilderness and were kept safe during the three and a half-year Jewish War. It is this passage which shows us the precise meaning of a 'time' — that is, a year of three hundred and sixty days.

Let us see if we can establish further the exact relationship between the three and a half times of Revelation and that of Daniel. Daniel is describing particular events of history, namely the persecution of Antiochus Epiphanes and the war of the Jews against the Romans. Since he is describing certain specific events, the distinction between 1260 days and 1290 days, for example, is important. But they are important apply so far as those particular events are concerned. As applied to the present age the distinction is unimportant. These past periods of time (both of approximately three and a half years) are simply *types* of the present age, and particularly of the period preceding the second advent. We shall consider the relevance of Antiochus's persecution when we look at the following chapter. In the present chapter it is the Jewish War which is relevant. Now the 'three and a half times' of Revelation 12 is exactly equivalent to that of Daniel 12:7. The 'three and a division times' of Daniel 7:25 is approximately equivalent, but not exactly. This tends to confirm our interpretation of Daniel 12:7. For various reasons we thought it likely that Daniel was speaking of the Jewish War with Rome. In Revelation we find an exactly similar term used in connection with a scene which has strong associations with this same Jewish War. As far as the present age is concerned the minutiae of these three and a half years are unimportant; but they assume considerable importance when we try to identify the specific historical events Daniel was predicting.

We read these words in Daniel 12:7: 'I heard him swear by him who lives for ever that it would be for a time, two times, and half a time; and that when the shattering of the power of the holy people comes to an end all these things would be accomplished'. These words primarily refer to the end of the old dispensation; but in line with the use Revelation makes of the Jewish War, we can, perhaps, apply them in a secondary sense to the present dispensation. In Daniel's time 'the holy people' referred to the Jews. In our time it refers to the worldwide church. The old era of Jewish nationhood ended with the three and a half-year war against Rome. The present era of the church will come to an end after the symbolical 'three and a half years' of war with the world. In the case of the Jews the war ended 'when the shattering of the power of the holy people came to an end'. Revelation 11 informs us that at the end of the age the world will appear to break the power of the church — and this will indeed be the end, because Christ will then return.

The fifth beast

We are told that the dragon 'was angry with the woman, and went off to make war on the rest of her offspring, on those who keep the commandments of God and bear testimony to Jesus'. The dragon's instrument, in his persecution of Christians, is a great beast.

> 'And I saw a beast rising out of the sea, with ten horns and seven heads, with ten diadems upon its horns and a blasphemous name upon its heads. And the beast that I saw was like a leopard, its feet were like a bear's, and its mouth was like a lion's mouth. And to it the dragon gave his power and his throne and great authority.' (Revelation 13:1, 2)

It is immediately obvious that this picture is drawn from Daniel. Note that the beast John saw is a combination of the four beasts of Daniel 7. It is like a leopard, but it has the feet of a bear and the mouth of a lion, and it has ten horns. In addition, it has all the seven heads of Daniel's four beasts. The latter beasts represented great earthly empires, great anti-God organisations of Man. They are combined in the beast of Revelation to represent all human governments and secular organisations which oppose and persecute the church during this present age. In its widest sense, indeed, the beast represents godless society as a whole. In the days of the early church this primarily meant the Roman empire — and the narrative itself hints at this very strongly. In chapter 17 we see a woman seated on the seven heads of a similar ten-horned beast. The narrative indicates clearly that she represents the city of Rome, and that the seven heads represent the 'seven hills' on which it was built ('the seven heads are seven mountains on which the woman is seated . . . and the woman that you saw is the great city which has dominion over the kings of the earth').

Now the beast represents governments and organisations which oppose the church during *this* age. At least three of Daniel's beasts represent empires of the previous age. In other words, these empires of the past *typify* the powers which oppose the church during the present age. If three, why not four? It is logical, surely that *all four empires* are empires of the previous age. They are combined into one ferocious beast to typify all the powers which oppose and persecute the church during the present age. The beast of Revelation is a combination of *all* Daniel's four beasts, and yet at the time of the vision it appeared to represent the Roman empire. It is surely unlikely that one of the original four beasts was this same Roman empire. It is more sensible to assume that the beast of Revelation *follows after* the four beasts of Daniel. Those beasts belonged to the old age. In other words, the four beasts of Daniel represent Babylon, Media, Persia and Greece of the old era. The beast of Revelation represents Rome and all other anti-God powers of the present era. These latter powers are *typified* by the four great heathen pre-Christian empires.

Now we read that the beast was given authority to continue 'forty-two months'. Here again we meet our period of three and a half years. We read also that 'it was allowed to make war on the saints and to conquer them'. Clearly this picture is derived from the persecutions of Antiochus Epiphanes as described by Daniel. The three and a half-year persecution of Antiochus typifies the persecution of Christians throughout the present age. We may add that he could further typify some specific antichrist who will arise shortly before the Lord's second advent. Revelation indicates that persecution will greatly increase towards the end of the age, and it seems likely that some particularly awful antichrist will make his or its appearance at this time (see also II Thessalonians 2:1—12).

As Christ's first advent was preceded by the persecutions of Antiochus, so His second advent will be preceded by the persecutions of the last and most terrible antichrist.

John next records that he saw 'another beast which rose out of the earth; it had two horns like a lamb and it spoke like a dragon'. A dragon in sheep's clothing! This beast deceives people into serving the first beast, and is called the false prophet. It is apparent that it represents false religions and false philosophies — in other words, false ideologies. Some people think that all religions lead to God. They have been deceived by the lamb-like appearance of the beast!

In chapter 14 we read of the blessing attending those who remain faithful to God and the punishment which awaits those who serve the beast. John then sees a vision of the 'harvest' at the end of the world. We have again been brought right through to the end of the age.

In chapters 15 and 16 we read of the seven bowls of wrath. As each bowl is poured out, John sees scenes symbolising God's judgments. God has been judging and punishing men throughout the age; but a last great judgment awaits the world. Although the various visions in Revelation deal with the whole age, there is an element of progression. The closer we come to the end of the book, the more the emphasis is on the events at the end of the age.

In chapter 17 John sees the vision of the great harlot sitting on the heads of the beast. The narrative hints very strongly that the woman specially symbolises the city of Rome with all its worldly, godless pleasure and its persecution of the saints. And Rome, like Babylon, typifies all worldly pleasure, and the godless way of life in general. Woven into the description of the woman and the beast, there are unmistakable references to Nero and Domitian, the terrible persecuting Roman emperors. Together with Antiochus Epiphanes, they typify all antichrists, particularly the final one at the end of the age.

Wilcock rather plays down the allusions to Rome — without entirely denying them — and concentrates on showing that the beast represents godless society as a whole. The harlot, like the second beast of chapter 13, is shown to represent false ideology. No doubt the symbols do point to these things, but the way in which they appear to describe Rome is surely more than a mere coincidence. The early Christians not only *saw* Rome in the descriptions of the harlot and the beast — they were *meant* to see this. The fact is that Rome (the empire and the city) was itself a symbol of godless society and false ideology.

In chapter 18 we read that the harlot is eventually destroyed by the beast itself. In chapter 19, by contrast, we read of the marriage supper of the Lamb, His bride being the church. Again we have been brought to the end of the age.

In the second half of the chapter we see Christ in His role of conqueror, wielding His 'rod of iron'. This He has been doing throughout the age. Again and again he has punished and destroyed the kings of the earth. We read in verse 16, 'On his robe and on his thigh he has a name inscribed, *King of kings and Lord of lords'*. In Daniel 8:25 the angel said that Antiochus Epiphanes 'shall even rise up against the *Prince of princes;* but, by no human hand, he shall be broken'. Here in Revelation 19:11—16 (and in 17:14) it is clearly indicated that the 'Prince of princes' who struck Antiochus (and the Greek empire) down, was Jesus Christ Himself. This strongly supports our suggestion that Daniel's fourth kingdom was destroyed by the pre-incarnate Christ. Colossians 1:15—17 indicates that He has had authority over the kingdoms of this world since the beginning of creation.

The climax comes in verses 19—21, where we see the beast gathering the forces of the world against the King of kings. This again pictures the world's final effort at the end of the age to destroy Christ and His church. We read, however, that the beast and the false prophet will be taken and 'thrown alive into the lake of fire'.

The dragon bound and destroyed

At this point the narrative returns to the dragon. John tells us that he saw an angel come down out of Heaven, bind the dragon 'for a thousand years', throw him into the pit and shut him in. This was done 'that he should deceive the nations no more, till the thousand years were ended. After that he must be loosed for a little while'.

We are reminded here of Christ's declaration that the gospel

must be preached in the whole world for a testimony to all
nations, and that Satan must first be bound before his goods
are spoiled (Matthew 24:14; 12:29). Christ implied that
Satan had been bound already, and so it would appear that
the 'thousand years' symbolises the age in which we are living
now. We are told that Satan was to 'deceive the nations no
more'. 'The nations' is a term which signifies the *Gentiles.*
Before the Christian era, Satan kept the Gentiles in the darkness of ignorance, with no knowledge of the true God. But
from the time of Christ's first advent, the light of truth has
been made freely available to all.

> 'And he will destroy on this mountain the covering that is
> cast over all peoples, the veil that is spread over all nations.'
> (Isaiah 25:7)

> '. . . I will give you as a light to the nations, that my salva-
> tion may reach to the end of the earth.' (Isaiah 49:6)

The question immediately arises, how can we reconcile
this picture of Satan's imprisonment with the earlier picture of
his persecuting the church and with other evidence that he is
active in the world today? Part of the answer is that the
pictures in Revelation are symbolical only and cannot deal
with all aspects of the truth. They describe a complex
spiritual situation which cannot be portrayed in a single
picture.

The two pictures of Satan describe two facts about his con-
dition today. Firstly, he is very active. Secondly, despite his
activity he has already been defeated by Christ and is in a
certain sense bound and helpless. The first picture shows Satan
actively persecuting the church. The second picture shows that
he is bound and helpless to prevent the spread of the gospel
to every nation of the world. This must have been very
reassuring to the early Christians who first read the book of
Revelation — and they were able to see its truth for themselves. They were experiencing Satan's activity through the
fearful persecutions of Rome, but they were also witnessing his
inability to prevent the spread of the gospel to the four
corners of the earth.

It is sometimes suggested that the angel with the great
chain who bound Satan is a picture of Christ Himself. If this

'angel' is Christ, we can be sure that the 'archangel' Michael also is a picture of Christ.

In verses 4 to 6 we read about the saints living and reigning with Christ for a thousand years, and we are told that this is the 'first resurrection'. We have had occasion to mention this section twice already, once in connection with the reign of the saints in Daniel 7:22, 27, and once in connection with the awaking of 'many of those who sleep in the dust of the earth' in Daniel 12:2.

We read in verse 4, 'Then I saw thrones, and seated on them were those to whom judgment was committed', and in Daniel 7:22 (R.V.) we read that 'judgment was given to the saints of the Most High; and the time came that the saints possessed the kingdom'. Comparison with Ephesians 1:18—2: 6, Revelation 1:5, 6 and 5:9, 10 (R.V.) makes it clear that the saints are reigning *now*. The question is whether the reign of the saints and the first resurrection applies only to those who have died and gone to be with Christ, or whether it includes those who have not yet died.

We read in verse 4 that those who reigned with Christ were 'the souls of those who had been beheaded for their testimony to Jesus . . . and who had not worshipped the beast or its image . . .'. In verse 5 we read that 'the rest of the dead did not come to life until the thousand years were ended'. The impression one gets is that John is speaking of those who have died. On the other hand, passages such as John 5:21, 24, 25, Ephesians 2:6, Revelation 1:6 and 5:9, 10 (R.V.) suggest that those who are still alive can be included. If the latter is the case, 'the first resurrection' would refer to the spiritual rebirth of a person as a Christian, when he or she passes 'from death to life' (John 5:24). Perhaps the most we can say is that Revelation 20:4—6 definitely does refer to the saints who have died, but it *may* also include those who are still alive.

We are told that Satan is to be loosed again after the thousand years and that he will gather the nations together against 'the camp of the saints and the beloved city' (the church — Hebrews 12:22). This goes with Revelation 19:19 which says, 'I saw the beast and the kings of the earth with their armies gathered to make war against him who sits upon the horse (Christ) and against his army'. It again appears that there will be a period of greatly increased apostasy, spiritual darkness and persecution of the church at the end of this age.

However, we are told that fire shall come down out of heaven and burn up those gathered against the church (the second advent — II Thessalonians 1:7—10); and Satan shall be cast into the lake of fire together with the beast and the false prophet. Earth and heaven shall pass away and the dead (unredeemed) shall be judged and cast, together with death and Hades, into the lake of fire. Then shall God create a new heaven and a new earth and He shall dwell with His saints for ever. What a glorious hope for those who put their trust in Christ!

Superficially, Revelation 20 seems to indicate a future millennium. However, scripture must always be interpreted in the light of other relevant scriptures — particularly in the case of such an obscure and difficult book as Revelation. Revelation is highly figurative, and must be interpreted in the light of the plain, straightforward teaching of the gospels, the Acts and the epistles. Figurative, symbolical and obscure scriptures should be interpreted in the light of scriptures which are written in straightforward, non-figurative language and can be clearly understood — *and not vice versa.* And this applies to the Old Testament as well as the New Testament. We must remember, too, that we are now in the new, Messianic age — not the old age, when 'Israel' meant the Jews. Christ's body, the church, is the true Israel; and it is we, who are 'children of Abraham by faith', who have inherited most of God's promises.

Christ Himself never gave any hint of a millennial age interposed between this age and the end of the world. He always indicated that this present age will be brought to a close by His own return for His saints and the casting into fire of those who are not His — e.g. the parable of the tares (Matthew 13:36—42). The New Testament writers indicate quite clearly that we are now in the 'thousand years' of Revelation and are looking forward *not* to an earthly millennial kingdom, but to something far more wonderful — a new heaven and a new earth. Let us take, for example, a passage in II Peter.

'. . . scoffers will come in the last days with scoffing . . . saying, "Where is the promise of his coming?" . . . the heavens and earth that now exist have been stored up for fire, being kept until the day of judgment and destruction of ungodly men . . . with the Lord one day is as a thousand years, and a thousand years as one day . . . the day of the Lord will come like a thief, and then the heavens will pass away with a loud noise, and the elements will be dissolved with fire, and the earth and the works that are upon it will be burned up . . . what sort of persons ought you to be in lives of holiness and godliness, waiting for and hastening the coming of the day of God, because of which the heavens will be kindled and dissolved, and the elements will melt with fire! But according to his promise we wait for new heavens and a new earth in which righteousness dwells.' (II Peter 3:3—13)

This passage from Peter's second letter provides very strong evidence that the 'thousand years' of Revelation 20 symbolises the age in which we are living now. In fact it acts as a very clear commentary on this part of Revelation. To start with, Peter eliminates any idea of a future millennium by indicating apostasy, followed by the destruction of the universe by fire and the creation of a new earth and universe. These are precisely the events which Revelation 20 and 21 say will terminate the 'thousand years'. And as if that were not enough, Peter speaks in this context of 'a thousand years' being as a day (and vice versa) with the eternal God. In the present writer's opinion, the 'thousand years' of Revelation 20 clearly refers to the present age, and is meant to convey the idea of a period of time that is long by human standards.

We are not saying that the early Christians expected a delay of many hundreds of years before Christ's return. Most of them probably expected something shorter than this — although Christ did indicate that there would be a considerable delay (Matthew 24:3—14; 25:5, 19; Luke 12:45; 21:24). But God is the ultimate author of the Bible, and the writers did not always appreciate the full significance of what they were writing. And this is something we need to remember when we study the book of Daniel.

In Daniel's case, God did not reveal that the Messiah's kingdom would be consummated many hundreds of years after its foundation. Daniel saw that the kingdom of Heaven would one day fill the whole earth and have absolute dominion; but he did not foresee the long period of time involved. As remarked in an earlier chapter, it is as if Daniel were gazing at a range of mountains from a great distance. From a distance they seemed to stand very close together. In the book of Revelation we are actually standing among these mountains and we can see that they stand far apart.

The last recorded words that Daniel spoke are these: 'O my lord, what shall be the issue of these things?' (12:8). The answer was not given until some six hundred years later. A large part of this answer is found in the book of Revelation. The books of Daniel and Revelation are in fact rather like the first and second instalments of a serial. The climax of Daniel's visions is the heavenly scene of Daniel 7, where the 'one like a son of man' is brought before the Ancient of Days and given power and dominion. The prophecies of Revelation *begin* with this scene (chapters 4 and 5), the scene of Christ's coronation following His death and resurrection. Daniel describes the old age, but points to a new age, the Messianic age. Revelation describes the new, Messianic age, but points to the end of the world, with the creation of a new heaven and a new earth.

Conclusion

We have dealt in this book with some things that are truly miraculous. The amazing prophecies of Daniel are among the many signs that God has given mankind — signs that confirm Christ's words, 'I am the way, and the truth, and the life; no one comes to the Father, but by me'. Let no one say that the evidence for the truth of these words is inadequate.

We read that the disciples' hearts burned within them as Jesus 'interpreted to them in all the scriptures the things concerning himself'. May our hearts also burn within us as we see the wonders of God's infinite might and majesty, love and compassion. He who is the great I AM, whose hand laid the foundation of the earth and whose right hand spread out the heavens loved us and gave Himself for us. Because our sins have separated us from Him, God the Son put aside His glory and out of eternity came into time. He came into this world as a man and Himself bore the penalty for our sins on the cross.

> 'For God so loved the world that he gave his only Son, that whoever believes in him should not perish but have eternal life.' (John 3:16)

As well as bearing witness to the Messiahship of Jesus, the prophecies of Daniel convey to us today the same message that they conveyed to the Jews who were persecuted by Antiochus Epiphanes — the message that although godless man may appear to be all-powerful, God is in control and His ultimate victory is certain.

It may well be that the worldwide church is due to enter — in the not very distant future — a period of great persecution. A period when the forces of evil will seem to triumph, and the Christian church will seem to be destroyed. But the message of Daniel's prophecies is as true now as it was over two thousand years ago. *God is in control.* In His own time He will destroy the kingdoms of this world — finally and completely — and then, at that time, His everlasting kingdom will indeed 'fill the whole earth'.

Further Evidence for a Sixth Century Date of Authorship

The following lines are quoted, with permission, from *Bible Men of Faith,* by J. Oswald Sanders (H.E. Walter, 1982), page 66.

'Other lines of evidence of the historicity of Daniel, as adduced by the late Professor R.D. Wilson of Princeton, are these: He is twice mentioned by Ezekiel,[1] who was carried off to Babylon about eight years after Daniel.

The first book of Maccabees presupposes the existence and common knowledge of the book of Daniel prior to the Maccabean age. In chapter two specific reference is made to Daniel and his three friends, who are grouped with such historical characters as Abraham and David.

That the Jews believed Daniel to have written long before Antiochus Epiphanes, appears from the story of Josephus, of the high priest Jaddua's encounter with Alexander the Great. When Alexander came to Jerusalem, the high priest sought to placate him by showing him the prophecy of Daniel that a king of Greece should overthrow Persia.'

Professor Wilson mentions three different authors who referred to Daniel by name. The first is Ezekiel, who wrote of Daniel's righteousness and wisdom, and his unlocking of secrets. Needless to say, many scholars do not accept that Ezekiel was referring to his contemporary in Babylon. However, Ezekiel's 'Daniel' was obviously a man of very great renown, so it is extremely unlikely that all memory of him was subsequently lost to the Jews. Yet this is precisely what we have to maintain if we say that Ezekiel was not referring to the man of the book of Daniel.

The second author is the writer of I Maccabees. This man wrote in about 103 B.C., only sixty years after the death of Antiochus Epiphanes — so his life may well have overlapped that of Antiochus. Clearly he was in a much better position than we are to judge whether Daniel was an historical person or an invention of the second century B.C. He quoted from the book of Daniel and regarded Daniel as fully historical.

The third author is Josephus, who was born in 37 or 38 A.D. He fully accepted that Daniel was an historical person and was the author of the book which bears his name.

As well as providing direct evidence for the genuineness of the book of Daniel, these facts confirm that when Jesus referred to 'the prophet Daniel', He was thinking of a sixth century prophet, and not of some unknown writer living in the second century B.C. (see 'Jesus and Pseudonymity', pp. 12-14).

---

1. Ezekiel 14:14-20; 28:3. Ezekiel spelt his name in a slightly different way — Dani'el rather than Daniy'el. But this does not matter, for in personal names the vowel letters were in free variation with one another, just as Do'eg (I Samuel 21:7; 22:9) was spelt Doyeg only a few verses later (22:18, 22). See 'Daniel' in *The Illustrated Bible Dictionary,* Inter-Varsity Press.